The Healthy Grape

A Beginner's Guide to Growing Grapes and Making Wine

Written by
P. Sharpley

All Rights Reserved © 2010 P. Sharpley

Disclaimer and Terms of Use: No information contained in this book should be considered as physical, health related, financial, tax, or legal advice. Your reliance upon information and content obtained by you at or through this publication is solely at your own risk. The author assumes no liability or responsibly for damage or injury to you, other persons, or property arising from any use of any product, information, idea, or instruction contained in the content provided to you through this book.

TABLE OF CONTENTS

CHAPTER 1 – STARTING THE VINEYARD............5

CHAPTER 2 – PLANTING 19

CHAPTER 3 – TRELLIS..31

CHAPTER 4 – EARLY VINEYARD CARE 41

CHAPTER 5 – VINEYARD MANAGEMENT...........53

CHAPTER 6 - THE START 67

CHAPTER 7 – PICKING GRAPES FOR WINE.......79

CHAPTER 8 – BASICS OF WINE MAKING...........87

CHAPTER 9 – MAKING WHITE WINES 99

CHAPTER 10 – MAKING RED WINES 107

CHAPTER 11 – ELEVAGE 117

CHAPTER 12 – BOTTLING................................ 125

CHAPTER 13 – TYPES OF WINES 133

Part I – THE VINEYARD

Chapter 1 – Starting the Vineyard

Grapes have been cultivated for thousands of years. Viticulture, also known as cultivation of grapes, is a long and hard process. However, as with anything, planning and adequate preparation will pave the way for an enjoyable and exciting experience

A vineyard is a macro universe in itself. Managing one is a task that requires an almost omniscient knowledge of grape facts. However, this is not impossible. A major initial decision for grape growers to make is where to locate their vines in relation to the limitations of their chosen property's boundaries. Within this framework, the vine grower must review and compare environment considerations such as:

- ✓ daily sunlight duration
- ✓ slope
- ✓ altitude
- ✓ frost
- ✓ heat pockets
- ✓ spacing
- ✓ soil quality
- ✓ rainfall trends
- ✓ water drainage
- ✓ wind
- ✓ climate trends

Certain grape varieties can only be successfully grown in the correct geographic location, where climate and soil conditions are appropriate to the variety you would like to cultivate. Thus, while there are other equally-important factors to consider, determining the correct location is critical; this is an irreversible decision and will spell the difference between a successful, long-lived vineyard and a disastrous, short-lived one.

Selecting the orientation of the site is a decision to be made by the individual grower. This could be based not only on the inherent topography of the site, but could well be motivated by market conditions since it involves extending or shortening the growing season. A South-facing slope gives an earlier crop, but there is more danger of injury to the tender shoots from late spring frost. With northern or eastern facing slopes this risk is avoided, but gives a later harvest. For the grower, the decision to make is whether an earlier crop is worth the risk.

- There are also other external considerations such as the matter of cost, proximity to markets, labor supply, availability of water, etc. These factors will determine the profitability of the venture and crucial to its very survival.

- The amount of sunlight available, the extent and variety of the surrounding flora and fauna, soil condition and prevailing climate are also important factors to consider when planning where to start the vineyard.

- The growing season must coincide with the time when sunlight is most abundant. Pests and other animals that could destroy the crops must be controlled so it is important that the vineyard is located far from where these creatures reside. Soil composition must be analyzed so it can be matched with the correct vine type too.

General climatic conditions will dictate how the whole process will proceed.

> A site that has a gentle slope and good drainage will make the best location. It should not be near any woodlands or overgrown areas, where wildlife could eat grapes and damage vines. The vineyard should not be located near farms that may be using herbicides that are harmful to the vines.

While modern technology could enhance the process of wine production, its presentation, even marketing and other economic considerations; only the best-located and best-prepared vineyard can produce the best wines.

SELECTING THE VINE

You need to know your agricultural zone rating first before you can successfully select vines for propagating.

✓ A zone rating is a number assigned to a specific region of land. There are several factors that come into making this determination. One of those factors is average minimum temperature.

On detailed maps, you can see zones subdivided into "a" and "b" classifications, with "a" being zones with cooler conditions. A plant rating of zone 5 to 9, for example, indicates an ability to adapt to climatic conditions existing in those zones. Your county USDA Extension Service can provide you with the latest and most accurate assessment.

Knowing the length of the average growing season for your area will help you to make a good decision in choosing which vine to cultivate. While soil condition could be improved and adjusted, weather conditions, on the other hand, are quite permanent and you would always remain at its mercy. So being armed with the correct knowledge of which varieties are proven to be suited to your climate zone rating will help improve your odds of being successful.

All types of grapes require enough sunlight, water and care. You will have more success in growing grapes if you select and plant a variety that thrives in your climate. Selecting otherwise will only end in disaster.

- ✓ The wine maker may be skilled, but the total quality of the wine is determined by the quality of the grapevine.

Your choice of the varieties to plant is also dependent on what kind of wine you want to make. Are you going to make white wine or red wine? The choice depends mainly on your personal tastes and preferences and the market you want to cater to.

Of the three major species of grapes used in wine production worldwide, the Vitis vinifera is the most popular species – used in 99% of the world's wine. Estimates say that there are thousands of varieties of this species: some of the best known are Cabernet Sauvignon, Chardonnay, Chenin Blanc, Merlot, Pinot Noir, Riesling, Sauvignon Blanc, Syrah, and Zinfandel. A long, hot growing season and a mild winter is required to grow this vine, but it is a fairly hardy strain that is possible to grow across nearly all of North America.

Another vine commonly grown in North America, mainly in the northeastern US and Canada, is Vitis Larusca. The Concord grape comes from this species but it is generally regarded inferior as a winemaking species because it is believed to impart a musky quality to wines that aficionados do not like.

Vitis rotundifolia (or Muscadine) is the third major species of grape used for wine making. Florida uses it a lot because of the warm and humid climate there that this species requires. Muscadines produce a somewhat sweet wine - good for dessert wine – and according to research, provides better antioxidant health benefits than other red wines.

Wines can also be a product of multiple species. Blending grapes can produce excellent wines such as the Northern Italian blend of cesanese, sangiovese and montepulciano from Lazio and Tuscany.

Another important consideration to include in selecting the vine is the rootstock. It is the lower portion of the vine that is responsible for reproduction and disease fighting. It anchors the plant and is the conduit of the soil nutrients going up the plant. It is essential to plant roots because of the differences in soil environment. This is easily done these days as technology has made it possible to match soil samples to rootstock ensuring greater chance of success. Most reputable nurseries will guarantee their supply of rootstock.

CLIMATE AND GEOGRAPHY

Climate is an indispensable part of the site where the vineyard is located. It is the single most important factor that influences the quality of wine grapes and how it is preserved. Hot and cold climates can affect wine quality to the point of spoilage and outright disaster. You must be sure to select grape varieties that ripen during the growing season. As much as possible, you should avoid growing grape varieties that mature during the hot summer months.

The likelihood of dangerously low spring or winter temperatures should be one important element to be considered for site suitability. You should avoid areas known for excessive or frequent temperature shifts, such as those with early spring/fall frost and sustained low winter temperatures. The same factors should also be considered when deciding on the altitude of the site, as frost settles in low-lying areas first and for a longer duration. A slope oriented towards the south is warmer, as it gets more sun and, thus, usually yields better results. A vineyard on an eastern- facing slope dries faster in the morning following dew or rain. This could reduce disease problems. North facing slopes have vines whose buds break in the spring but will be colder in the fall.

There are three climatic factors that should be considered essential:

1. **Climate of the region** – the macro climate - refers to the regional minimum winter temperatures and summer temperatures range and humidity.

2. **Climate of the site in question** – the meso climate - refers to the specific location– the slope and the moderating effect of body of water.

3. **Climate of the grapevine itself** – the micro climate - refers to the specific area, like area inside a canopy or around a cluster

The growing season at the determined site should be long enough for the vine to mature. Ensuring that enough sunlight is available all through out the season will help ripen the fruit and the vine itself. The rooting zone must provide correct amounts of essential mineral elements in order to produce healthy vines. Non-essential mineral elements may pose problems if they are toxic, both to the plants and the people surrounding them. Sufficient water supply should also be present, neither lacking nor in over-supply, as the grapevine roots will suffer root rot. Where vines are not irrigated, the soil must be able to retain enough moisture in the root zone to provide what the vines need between rains.

TYPES OF GRAPES

Winemaking requires a clear understanding of the types of grapes to be used because different grape types manifest different individual characteristics. Grapes come from two main families – Vitis Vinifera, which is prevalent in Europe; and Vitis Labrusca, which is common to Canada and the eastern United States. There are over 5,000 varieties of wine grapes with the following main types:

- **Auxerrois** – Also known as Malbec or Cot, Auxerrois, is the grape of choice for a neutral wine that is fruity and soft. This variety is mainly grown in Canada and Luxembourg. In the Alsace region of France, Auxerrois is often blended with the Pinot Blanc grape.

- **Barbera** – Is a low-tannin grape characterized by a tarry flavor. It is a widely-planted variety of grape. In California, Barbera equals Merlot grape vines in acreage, while it has more area planted in Italy than Sangiovese and Nebbiolo.

- **Cabernet Franc** – Is a parent of the Cabernet Sauvignon grape. It is known as Breton in the Loire Valley of France; also known as Bouchy, Bouchet, Gros Bouchet, and Veron. Cabernet Franc is mostly used as an additive to enhance other grapes.

- **Cabernet Sauvignon** – This type of grape creates Cabernet Sauvignon wines which tend to taste like blackberries and cedar. On the vine, these grapes are red, small, and tough. Grown extensively in California and Australia, the grape contains a lot of tannin which leads to a good red wine once properly aged.

- **Chardonnay** – Grown in Burgundy, Champagne, California, Australia, and South Africa, Chardonnay is a fresh fruity grape whose wine tends to taste like fruits – melon, peach, etc. It is one of the most popular and easiest to grow white grapes; the buds grow early and easily and have high ripeness levels.

- **Chennin Blanc** – Planted primarily in the US and in the Loire valley of France, Chennin Blanc grapes make a light, fruity wine. It is also known as White Pinot (Pinot Blanco) and Steen in South Africa.

- **Cinsaut** – Considered the parent of pinotage, it is grown in Southern France, Lebanon, Australia and South Africa. This grape is used mostly for blending with other stronger varieties of grapes.

- **Colombard** – Used in South Africa and other countries, these grapes create wine with tropical fruit overtones, a light wine that goes well with seafood. It is also used by South Africans to make brandy.

- **Cortese** – Grown primarily in the Piedmont region of Italy, this is the primary grape for Gavi wine. This grape ripens early and makes a neutral white wine.

- **Ehrenfelser** – It is a cross between the Johannisberg Riesling grape and Sylvaner grape clone. Ehrenfelser is extremely frost resistant and it creates a wine that tastes like Riesling wine. It is grown primarily in Canada.

- **Gamay** – This grape is used in Beaujolais Nouveau wine. The wine is a light fruity red and the grapes are grown in France.

- **Gewurztraminer** - It is a German variety that is also widely grown in Italy, California, Canada, and Australia. The wine created has a floral taste with nutty tones.

- **Grande Vidure** – This grape, also known as Carmenere, is best known for its use in Medoc wines. This variety produces low yields and has problems with coloure and oidium.

- **Grenache** – This grape, widely grown in France, Spain, and California is most often used for rose wine. It is the second most planted grape in the world. Wines from Grenache tend to be sweet and fruity, with little tannin. Grenache refers to Grenache Noir, the red variety; although, there is also a Grenache Blanc.

- **Kerner** – It is a German cross of the Reisling grape and Black Hamburg. It is frost resistant and grows well in cooler climates. The wine from Kerner is sweet like the Reisling wine. It is grown in the Michigan area of the US where the climate is cool.

- **Lemberger** – Known also as Blaufrankish and Limberger, Lemberger is a popular Austrian grape wine that is also grown extensively in Washington State of the US.

- **Marechal Foch** – This grape has very small berries in small clusters that ripen early with hardy vines that make a good range of red wines.

- **Merlot** – Merlot is a major blending component of most Bordeaux wines that is grown in France, Italy, Australia, and in California, Washington and Long Island, NY. This is an early ripening grape with gentle flavors of cherry, honey, and sometimes mint. It has less tannin than some of its red cousins.

- **Muller-Thurgau** – The most widely planted grape in Germany, it comes as a mix of Riesling and Sylvaner. It has a floral aroma. It is also grown in Austria, New Zealand and the northwest US.

- **Muscadet** – Muscadet of Muscadekke is a white grape grown in Bordeaux. It is not related to the Muscat grape and it has a grapey-tasting flavor. It is well known for use in the Tokay wine of Australia.

- **Muscadine** – It is a Muscadinia grape that is not part of the normal vinifera grapes branch. Largely grown in southeaster US and in Mexico, the Muscadine is a large grape with thick skin, is very hearty and grows in places that other grapes might not.

- **Muscat** – This is a very grapey-tasting grape that does not ripen easily and is used for Asti Spumanti, the sparkling wine from Italy. Varieties of Muscat include Muscat Blanc, Moscato, Muscat of Alexandria and Muscadel.

- **Muskat Krymskii** – Creates aromatic white wine that tends to be wheat-colored, and has a clean fruity bouquet. It is grown in Bulgaria, the Ukraine and other eastern European countries.

- **Nebbiolo** – Notoriously difficult to grow, this late-ripening grape is known to be tannic, pruny, tarry, and chocolaty. It is grown in the

Piedmont area of Italy, Switzerland, California, and Australia.

- **Optima** – A German variety of grape that is used to add sugar to other wines; it is not a very palatable variety on its own.

- **Ortega** – A cross between Muller Thurgau, Madeleine Angevine and Gewurtztraminer, Ortega is very flavorful and has a mangoey taste. It is grown in Canada.

- **Petite Sirah** – A dark, tannic, and fruity grape, it has smoky or chocolaty tones to it. It is popular in California where it is used in "jug wines".

- **Pinot Blanc** – It is a mutation of the Pinot Gris grape that is used in Californian sparkling wines. It has flavor very much similar to Chardonnay wine. It is grown in the Alsace region of France, Italy, and Austria where it is known as Weissburgunder.

- **Pinot Gris** – A clone of Pinot Noir, it is grown in France, Austria and along the west coast of the US. It can be used to create both fine whites and roses.

- **Pinot Noir** – Softer and earlier ripening than Cabernet grapes, Pinot Noir grapes are very sensitive to conditions. They are used in red wines and as a white ingredient in Champagne (used without skins). They are grown in Burgundy, Australia, California, Oregon, Italy and Germany.

- **Pinotage** – Was developed in the early 1900s and grown primarily in South Africa; it is mix between pinot noir and cinsaut. This grape makes a hearty wine, with fruit and spice taste.

- **Riesling** – It can produce a dry, crisp and fruity wine; also produces honeyed, musky flavors in warmer climates or when left longer on the vine. It is native to Germany, but also grown in France, Australia, California, and the Finger Lakes region of New York.

- **Sauvignon Blanc** – Grown primarily in California and France, this grape has a grassy flavor and makes a crisp, light wine.

- **Scheurebe** – A mix between Sylvaner and Johannisberg Riesling, this grape is mostly planted in Germany and is used to create aromatic white wines.

- **Semillon** – This grape, used mostly in Bordeaux, France, is thin-skinned and ripens early. It has a grassy, figgy flavor. It is also grown in Australia and California and is often blended with Sauvignon Blanc.

- **Seyval** – It is the most widely planted grape east of the Rocky Mountains in the US. It has melony flavors, as well as grassy/hay overtones.

- **Sylvaner** – Once a widely-planted variety in Alsace region of France, it has dwindled in popularity. The grape produces a pleasant, but bland, white wine with light spice and floral flavors.

- **Syrah/Shiraz** – Grown in France and in California as Syrah wine, and in Australia as Shiraz, this grape tends towards a minerally, blueberry, or sometimes spicy and peppery type of flavor. This should not be confused with Petite Sirah which is an entirely different grape.

- **Siegerrebe** – A cross between Gewurtztraminer and a normal table grape, it ripens very early and has high sugar content. Wines created from Siegerrebe has peach and honey taste.

- **Viognier** – Predominantly found in the Rhone Valley and in California, it is noted for spice, floral, citrus, apricot, apple and peach flavors. It produces medium-bodied wines with high acids and fruit. It can be used to produce highly complex wines.

- **Vidal Blanc** – Mostly grown in the northeast US, it is very hearty and does well in late-harvest, sweet wines, as well as in ice wines.

- **Zinfandel** – They are believed to have originated in Southern Italy but they are now largely grown in California. The wines created from Zinfandel grapes can be fruity or spicy, depending on age. When the skins are left on, Zinfandel makes Red Zinfandel wines, and when the skins are removed makes White Zinfandel wines.

Chapter 2 – Planting

PLANTING

Once the decision to go ahead and start a vineyard is reached, it is time to consider the steps that will lead to the actual production of grapes. After the general prevailing climate trends are considered; and it is determined where the vineyard will be located; and the inherent limitations of the property's boundaries are identified and ready to be altered and developed; it is now time to get your hands dirty. You need to:

- ✓ Choose the site,
- ✓ Determine what size is manageable for you,
- ✓ Have the soil type analyzed, and
- ✓ Select the matching grape stocks that are suitable for planting in your land.

The best time to start planting grapevines is early spring. Planting during fall is a poor choice because the plants are likely to be lost during the winter. The first year of planting should be spent preparing the soil and selecting the cultivars. Also during this time the vines are planted, mulched, fertilized and kept free of weeds, insects and diseases. Broken or dead portions of branches and roots are pruned off. The top growth of a single cane should also be pruned off. To keep them off the ground and make spraying more effective, vines are usually tied to a stake. Supplemental watering is advised if the season of planting is dry. As much as possible, you should do everything to ensure that you achieve the optimum first-year growth by using these practices.

CHOOSING A SITE FOR THE VINEYARD

The goal of establishing an ideal site for your vineyard is to have good grape-producing vines. You can only achieve this if you have the ideal site. As real estate agents have "location, location, location" as their battle-cry, so you should have it too. You need to know if you have all the right ingredients, such as the optimal altitude for growing, the right angle of the sun for the vine to receive the most benefits of sunlight, adequate availability of water and soil chemistry, to name a few. As a huge venture requiring a lot of capital, you need to provide the best environment of the vines to prosper and exist for many years.

EVALUATING THE SITE

The elevation of the land will affect the type of grapes you can grow on it. Grapes are sensitive to frost, thus, altitude should be taken into account. Be prepared to answer the following questions:

- Is the land prone to flooding?

- How much snow falls in the winter?

- The location must be higher than the surrounding area and could be irrigated properly. The site should have good internal soil drainage.

- Which side does the sun rise and set on the property?

- Is it on a slope so that you can position the plants in the correct orientation to get the right amount and length of exposure to the sun?

> How steep is the slope?

> Are you able to create "balconies" where you can plant the vines and still reach all of them with the tools or machinery you have?

Once you have planted your vines, it would be very difficult to alter and improve the physical properties of the soil. So it is imperative that you ensure that the foregoing have been determined to comply with the requirements of the type of grapes you want to grow. Otherwise, you may need to alter your plans of which types you want to plant or you may have to re-organize the land, or even worse, to relocate to suit your planting needs.

SIZE OF THE VINEYARD

Is the size you are considering available, and can it provide income that will cover all the costs you will incur and still generate some future earnings? With the skills you have or are planning to acquire, enable you be able to manage the size you have in mind? How about the supply of labor?

How big is the property you need to start a vineyard? The answer to this tricky question depends on how you plan to produce your wine and how well you are able to manage its marketing. Can you make a profit out of the amount of wine you are able to produce, bearing in mind the prevailing prices at the time of selling your product?

The size of your newly established vineyard can be changed later. You could decide in the future to extend its boundaries as soon as you see the need to do so. You can opt to buy neighbouring lands, or you could initially acquire a property larger than what you intended and expand when needed. Whatever the circumstances, you have several options open to explore. However, to get the most out of what you have and what is available, you have to get *the right land in the right place,* and make sure that it's potential to give you the crops you desire is present and you are able to take advantage of them.

SOIL TYPE AND PREPARATION

As discussed above, there are a lot of things you need to know and plan for when you are looking to establish a new vineyard. The location and cost of land and labor, of course, matter much; but you also need to know the type and quality of the soil and what can be planted in it.

Soil type. If you really want to be sure, the easiest way to know if the soil is suitable for planting a new vineyard is to have a professional test the soil. Acquire this service from an expert and get a clear idea of what type of grapes would be suitable to plant on the land.

- All good vineyard soils should have minerals that are vital to the health of the vines, including calcium that helps neutralize the soil pH levels.

- The presence of iron is essential too, as it is used for photosynthesis.

- Magnesium is also required as it is an important component of chlorophyll.

- To improve the vine's total health, nitrogen, which is assimilated in the form of nitrates, must be present; as well as, phosphates which encourage root development and potassium which improves the vine's metabolism.

For additional information you can contact the USDA Soil Conservation Service.

Soil drainage. Since it is through the soil that minerals and nutrients enter the vine, the land should have good internal soil drainage. An area of thin topsoil and subsoil that sufficiently retains water, but also has good drainage, is ideal. It is also desirable to have at least 30 inches of unobstructed soil depth.

- Rain water accumulating and displacing oxygen surrounding the root system will result in root rot.

- If this happens, vines will not be as vigorous and productive as they should be. To avoid this, good soil drainage must be ensured.

- A sign of good internal drainage includes bright, uniformly-yellowish-brown or brown subsoil.

- Subsoil having mottled or dark gray color usually indicates poor drainage. Tile drains can be installed if the general topography is favorable, yet drainage is poor.

The state of the soil's drainage system also affects the ability of the soil to retain heat and/or reflect it back to the vine, an important factor that affects the ripening of the grape.

Transition layers. A transition layer exists where the soil texture changes dramatically. An example is a layer that is all sand or all clay. The vine's roots cannot penetrate these layers. To make sure that they do, you must break through these layers and mix them before planting. An alternative is to just find a location where there are no transition layers. If that's not possible, you can reduce the effects of transition layers by ripping through one layer in opposite directions. You must rip the soil 3 or 4 feet deep on 3 foot centers to improve rooting depth and soil drainage.

Current vegetation. Weeds and grasses should be taken off the vineyard, but their growth indicates a good site. Where they are abundant, the soil is productive. But you must still check the rooting depth of these plants.

Soil texture. The mixture of sand, silt and clay together form the texture of the soil. Sand in the soil makes it look and feel grainy. It is important for drainage. Clay on the other hand causes soil particles to stick together and is important for water and nutrient retention.

Knowledge of these facts can help you in planning the irrigation and fertilization processes you need. With the correct management practices, vineyards with soil texture ranging from sandy loams to heavy clay and silty-clay loams can produce good vines.

Irrigation. As mentioned above, if the planting season is dry, supplemental irrigation should be initiated. It increases plant survival odds in the first two years. Mature vines are in constant need of moisture throughout summer for fruit growth. They also need water for fruit bud development for the following year's crop. Maintaining a well managed irrigation system will actually pay for itself in the early years of the vineyard.

Water quantity and quality. Normally, a vine requires a minimum of 5 gallons per day. However, a more adequate quantity would be 10 gallons per plant. This would provide needed water even during high stress. Water quality can be determined by testing a water sample for pH salinity (total dissolved salts), Na and Cl. A pH range of 5.5 to 7.5 is generally acceptable. Irrigation water salinity is not a problem if concentrations are below 640 ppm. To avoid toxicity problems, sodium and chloride levels need to be below 460 and 143 ppm respectively. Salinity is measured and reported in electrical conductivity (EC) I milli mhos per centimeter. Convert EC to ppm by multiplying by 640 ppm.

Air drainage. Spring frost damage to fruit buds, blossoms and small fruits after bloom will be avoided on vineyards planted on 2 to 3 percent slopes. As cold air moves down, it draws warmer air from higher layers. A vineyard planted in a low site, such as along a creek or at the bottom of a hill, is more susceptible to low temperature injury than a site in a higher area.

Avoid soil erosion. Sites having steep slopes will have more soil erosion. Such steep slopes also present more problems in the operation or use of machinery and other equipments. Cool temperatures on north facing slops may delay vine growth enough in the spring to avoid damage due to frost. Earlier spring growth with increased risk of frost injury may be present on a south facing slope.

Windbreak. Beginning a windbreak at least a year before planting is beneficial in areas with full exposure to summer winds. Protection from southwest winds can reduce vine damage and increase pest control.

ORDERING AND PLANTING GRAPE STOCKS

The most suitable sources of grape stocks are nurseries that specialize in grape plants and grow the desired cultivars.

- ➢ You should order at least 6 months to a year before planting to ensure delivery.

- ➢ The best ones are the one-year-old plants because they are healthy and have a well-developed, fibrous root system. These are usually dormant, rooted cuttings grown the previous summer. Vines such as these will grow rapidly in the vineyard; and because they bear more quickly, they will repay the extra cost earlier and give greater returns over a period of years.

- ➢ Nursery plants aged two years or more are often those that were too weak for selling at the end of one year and they may grow poorly in the vineyard.

When the planting stock arrives, immediately check the roots for moisture. If dry, moisten them. They should be kept in a humid location at 35° to 40° F and covered with moist sawdust if planting is to be delayed. You could also line them in a trench with soil covering the roots. To give the plant time to become well-established and grow new roots before temperatures and water requirements increase, it is recommended that planting be done in mid-to-late March. Planting during fall can be done, too, if nursery plants are available. However, plants grown in the vineyard and hardened off there will most likely survive harsh winter temperatures with less plant loss than those plants that were planted during fall.

HARDWOOD CUTTINGS

The most common method of propagation is hardwood cuttings. They can be made at anytime after leaf drop in the fall until the sap starts to flow in the spring. There is a better chance of obtaining good callus formation if cuttings are prepared in the fall or early winter. Good callus formation is critical to rapid root formation in the spring. You can also obtain good results by making the cuttings a week or two before the sap rises in the spring and setting them out immediately.

- Cuttings made out of straight, vigorous, well-matured, one-year old canes with well-developed buds are best.

- They should be about pencil-size or slightly larger with four buds 2-3 inches apart.

- The ideal completed cutting is about 8 to 12 inches long.

As soon as there is no danger of frost, and when the ground has become warm in the spring, the soil should be prepared carefully to a depth of 8-12 inches. The cuttings should be set in a row about 5-6 inches apart. They should be deep enough so that only the top bud protrudes above the ground. You must make sure that the soil is firm around the cutting.

- Weed control is essential and can be done by hand, with herbicide or black plastic. Irrigation is a must and required in most years.

- If plastic is used, soil must be prepared in ridges, covered with plastic and cuttings planted through the plastic.

- Rooted cuttings can be dug up in the fall, graded and stored either by setting the roots in a trench in well- drained soil or stored under moist conditions at 34°F.

LAYERING AND GRAFTING

Layering and grafting are sometimes used in grape propagation.

- Layering is used for certain varieties that do not root readily from cuttings.

- Grafting, on the other hand, is mainly used by nurseries to establish a cultivar on different rootstocks.

There are grape varieties that do not root readily. To propagate such a variety, the layering method is employed. In this method, a narrow trench about 10 to 15 inches deep is dug in early spring where a new plant is desired. A healthy cane originating close to the ground on a neighboring vine is bent down to the bottom of the trench and vertically back up to brings two or more tip buds above the soil surface. To hasten rooting, the cane opposite each underground bud is wounded before the trench is filled. When shoots emerge on the part of the cane connecting the new plant to the mother plant, they should be stripped as only the shoots from the buds of the protruding cane should be allowed to grow. The following spring, the rooted plants can be severed from the parent vine and set in their permanent location.

ROOTSTOCKS

There are grape growers who prefer not to take the risk of purchasing or growing a whole plant. To be safe, they use healthy rootstocks and then graft vines onto them as they desire. This provides an extra measure of control over the growth of the plant, since the quality and characteristics of the resulting fruit are so important.

Some of the primary reasons for using a rootstock are:

1. To provide resistance to phylloxera and nematode parasites on the root system,

2. To isolate the scion cultivar from soil-born virus diseases,

3. To induce vigorous growth in a replant situation, and to avoid varietal susceptibility to lime-induced chlorosis.

If you suspect that any of these situations apply to the planned vineyard site, rootstocks should be considered.

Chapter 3 – Trellis

TRELLIS

Grapevines, as with any type of vines, are not strong enough to support themselves. As such, they need some form of support in order to grow as productive and as healthy as possible. To fulfill this need, the vines need to be trained onto a trellis – a structure that provides support for the growing vine.

Positioned correctly, trellises can:

- ✓ Help the vines get the maximum amount of sun during the day,

- ✓ Reduce labor cost,

- ✓ Avoid delayed bearing,

- ✓ Minimize exposure to disease and develop a strong and straight trunk.

Grapes need sunlight in order to produce flowers which will develop into desirable grapes. They will be more productive when exposed to the maximum amount of sunlight than if they are allowed to grow in shady conditions. Plants need sunlight for photosynthesis, and in the leaves of grapes, it results in the production of sugars and other elements essential to the development of the best fruit.

Constructed properly, trellises facilitate increase in vine size, structure and canopy management. They make it easy to see what parts of the vines are in need of pruning and determine what clusters need to be removed in the cluster thinning process.

Fungal diseases hound grapevines. They wreak havoc under stagnant, moist air conditions. But with vines trained onto a trellis and coupled with proper canopy management, better airflow is established, thereby reducing exposure to fungal diseases; and because the fruit is not in direct contact with the soil, soil-born fruit rot is avoided. It also makes it easier for them to be sprayed with fungicides and insecticides more thoroughly and evenly.

In addition, vines trained on a trellis accommodate better weed control under the plant as weeds can be sprayed with herbicides more effectively with less concern of herbicide damage to the vines.

Furthermore, harvesting the grapes is easier if the trellises used are appropriately well-designed and strong. The trellis system to be used is mainly influenced the type of cultivars and by harvesting method to be employed. The trellis design for grapes to be harvested by machine is different from the one for grapes to be harvested by hand.

Matching the Trellis System with the Cultivars. The trellis system must be suited to the cultivar being grown in the vineyard. Most American, and many French-American hybrid cultivars, tend to have a downward growth habit. For this type of growth, the best trellis type to use is one with a high renewal zone. This type of trellis involves training the grape plant on to the top wire, at least 5 to 6 feet above the ground. This allows plenty of space for the vines to curtain downward and just reach the ground by the end of the growing season. It will be necessary to reorient horizontal shoots and to prevent shading of the renewal zones along the top wire.

European cultivars, on the other hand, have an opposite growth habit. They tend to go upright and so the best type of trellis to use is one with an upward vertical shoot positioning. Because the shoots originate from a mid or low wire cordon or cane, they are positioned vertically upward through a set of catch wires.

Vine Vigor. Another important factor to consider before deciding on the type of trellis to use is vine vigor. Soil structure and climatic conditions both play significant roles in predicting how vigorous vine growth will be.

An appropriately designed and managed trellis will produce large canopy surface area and relatively low canopy density. The canopy will have 2 to 3 layers of leaves and minimal shading, which should result in a top quality crop with high sugar content.

Predicting vine vigor is difficult if no previous history is available for the site; but if prior cropping history exists, this could be a relatively simple task. However, soil samples should still be taken as test results will provide guidance for fertilizer use and give a rough estimate of the vine-vigor potential of the site.

Reduction of yield per acre will result if potential vigor is overestimated and vines are spaced too far apart. On the other hand, underestimation and inadequate trellis space will result in shading and other associated problems occurring. You need to make the correct choice before constructing the trellises, as it is easier than making corrections later on.

TRELLIS TRAINING SYSTEMS

Different climate conditions, soil characteristics, vine characteristics, and varietals all contribute to the choices of trellis systems to be used in order to obtain the best grapes and, ultimately, the best wine.

Guyot Training. Named after Dr. Jules Guyot, a 19th century French scientist. This system is well suited for low-yield vineyards. It takes advantage of vines that tend to have low vigor owing to relatively infertile soils. This system is desirable for this type of vine because the plants tend to put the majority of its energy into reproduction (fruit bearing), rather than simply expanding. The basic Guyot design is relatively simple to manage, as it has the flexibility to be modified easily based on local conditions. One important advantage is that it produces small yields of high quality grapes.

From the trunk of the vine, usually two fruiting canes are trained to grow in opposite directions along guide wires that run just above the trunk. By clinging to catch wires located above the canes, new shoots that emerge from the canes are trained to grow upwards. For optimum spacing and exposure to sunlight, shoots can be manually placed and the fruit clusters can hang below the leaves. This adds the benefit of good air circulation and controlled exposure to sunlight.

Vertical Shoot Positioned Trellis. Often abbreviated to VSP, this system is designed to arrange shoots so that they will grow upwards across guide wires. The usual practice for fruiting canes is they are trained to grow in opposite directions along two levels of wire. As in the simpler

Guyot method, fruit hangs 3 o 4 feet off the ground and below the raft of vertically growing leaves.

Cordon Training. Used in the warmer growing regions of Washington and California. Through this training approach, an arm of the vine is allowed to permanently grow along a bottom guide wire, with shoots emerging from the arm and trained vertically along additional wires. The grape clusters are left hanging roughly in the middle of the canopy while the shoots are trained to droop over the top wire.

Geneva Double Curtain. This is a complex trellis design and is rarely seen in new vineyards. Each plant is made to grow two trunks, whose cordons are trained across twin guide wires at a relatively high level from the ground. Curtain-like shoots are allowed to grow hanging downward. The canopy is divided, thereby increasing overall exposure, yet minimizing canopy density.

Lyre or U Shaped Trellis. This design has the vine divided into two fruiting canes, each growing in opposite directions. Shoots are arranged to grow vertically upwards across wires threaded through a U-shaped support system. The result is a divided canopy having less density because the leaves and fruit are spread across two curtains. Sun exposure is increased and the fruit is open to air movement, yet protected from sunburn.

Umbrella Kniffin System. This system uses long canes (10 to 20 buds each) that originate from several spurs at or near the top of the trunk. Four to six canes are retained, bent over the top trellis wire and tied securely to the mid wire. To avoid damage to the tender buds during the tying process, pruning must be finished before bud swells begin.

But because cane pruning cannot be mechanized, this system results in higher labor cost.

HARDWARE FOR TRELLIS CONSTRUCTION

The best starting and most important point to consider in the construction of trellises is the foundation. As with any type of construction, some are standard while others are more unconventional. What counts is that they are functional. Most common is either the use of the H-brace system, or the end post put in at a 5 degree angle from the vertical with a "dead man" or other earth anchor.

As proven by experience, however, it is the soil condition that is often a more critical factor in the failure of end-post construction-- rather the choice of using an angled or vertical post. It is essential, nevertheless, that the end-post assembly be made of sturdy material. Some growers prefer at least an 8 inch diameter end post in either of the above mentioned systems.

There are other materials available to growers. There are those which are not economical, and even too time consuming to consider installing. Factors to consider in selecting materials are adequate strength and freedom from toxic substances to the vines and people in and around the vineyard.

Line Post. Line posts provide anchors for the trellis system. Two of the most common line post materials are landscape timbers or a steel T-post. Both have advantages and disadvantages. Landscape timbers are economical, but can break off and may rot in a short period of time.

Heavy vine and crop weight can bend steel posts, especially in heavy wind conditions. They are also known to sink into the ground. Other materials used are fiberglass poles, 4-inch treated fence posts and well pipe. Important considerations for these materials include availability, strength and price.

Wire. Use of high-tensile 12 ½ gage steel is a must. Lighter weight wires are not recommended.

Additional hardware needed includes springs, ratchets, earth anchors, cross arms, wire fasteners and wire splicers.

The required tools for trellis construction includes: fence pliers, spinning jenny, posthole digger, tamper, shovel and saw. Holes for the posts can be dug manually or driven to the ground using a driver. There are cases when posts driven to the ground have been more stable than those placed in the hole and tamped into the soil.

BASIC TRELLIS INSTALLATION

Posts. There are two types of support posts needed for a vineyard:

1. Heavy posts that are the main supports of the wire, and

2. Lighter support stakes for each vine.

Wood is the main material for the wire-support posts, while metal or wood is generally used for the vine supports. As much as possible, you need to use black locust, which is a rot-resistant wood, for wooden posts. It can last as long, or longer, than treated posts, and is free of chemicals that might leach into the soil. Other type of wood must be treated to prevent rot.

A minimum of 3 inches in diameter should be allowed for the wire support posts for rows up to 300 feet long. For longer rows, a larger diameter post should be used, up to about 6 inches in diameter. This is due to the increased weight of the wire and the greater pull on the posts. Depending on the type of system used, the number of wire support posts within the rows may be increased or lessened. A vineyard that is exposed to a lot of wind needs heavy support posts set as close as 20 feet apart to keep the row from leaning. This is especially true if the soil is wet.

In average soil, heavy wire support posts should be set at least 2 feet deep. At least 8 feet long posts are needed in order to leave 6 feet above the ground for the use of the trellis. If your land has soft soil, such as sand, you must use taller posts and set them deeper, or you can set them in cement for a firm anchor. If you have a very rocky soil instead, you can set the posts less deep, about 1½ feet deep for an 8 foot post. Posts are held more strongly in rocky ground than in other types of soft soils. The downside is you do more work in digging the hole for the post.

Wire. The heaviest wire size used to support grapevines is 12.5 gauge. The average size generally used is from 9 to 12 gauge. Wires are usually sold by weight rather than by length, with 100 pound rolls as the basic unit. You may be able to buy smaller amounts, but a cutting charge may be added so that it may be cheaper to buy the whole roll instead. Tempered, high-tensile, stainless steel is recommended, as it resists rust much better than other types such as galvanized steel, and stretches so little in its lifetime.

Wire Anchors. To support grapevines, wires must be stretched tightly. It is not sufficient to simply tie the wire to end posts. Some type of anchor is usually buried in the ground at each end of the row. The wire is attached to it or the end posts and solidly braced so that the wire can be stretched tightly. Using a commercial-type anchor is the easiest way to do this. This is a heavy iron rod 2 to 3 feet long, possessing a loop at one end and a split disk at the other.

If using wire anchors, posts must be set at an angle of about 15 degrees off vertical, pointing away from the row. This way, the posts are braced against the pull of the tightened wire.

Attaching The Wires. To attach the wire, drill two holes in the end posts at the appropriate height, making them parallel to the direction in which the wires are to run. Then drill another hole above those two at a 90-degree angle to them, parallel to the ground. The top hole is for the anchor.

Run wire through the hole in the top and down through the loop in the anchor. Do this twice so you have two strands through the hole. Pull up the slack and leave at least a foot or more overlapping in each direction. Twist the ends around and over each other and wrap them thoroughly. Nothing else needs to be done at this point. Repeat this at the other end of the row.

Stretching The Wire. To stretch the wire, take an end from the coil of wire and thread it through the lowest hole in the end post. As you feed out the wire, continue threading it through the posts all the way to the end of the row. At the far end, the wire should be threaded through the hole in the other end post and wrapped around to it at least twice. The wire should be wrapped one last time with at least 1 foot of it around itself, just in back of the point where it enters the hole.

Using the hand to pull the majority of the slack, hook the wire in the claw of a claw hammer right where it comes through the hole. To pull the wire tighter, you need to brace the head of the hammer against the post and rock it to one side. You need a second hammer to catch the wire right at the hole and repeat. You can stretch the wire quite tightly this way. You have to bend the wire around the post as you stretch it, and as it resists pulling back, you can wrap the wire all the way around the post to hold it. Finally, wrap the wire around to fix it in place.

Chapter 4 – Early Vineyard Care

TRAINING AND PRUNING

To create balance in fruiting and vegetative growth, 80 to 90 percent of the new wood in the grapevine must be removed. The ideal time to do the pruning is in the spring, while the vines are dormant. It should be done, preferably, a short time before the sap begins to circulate.

To facilitate understanding, we give the following definitions:

- Pruning is the removal of wood to regulate fruit production.

- Training is the removal of wood to shape the vine so it will bear a good crop without breaking, and will not interfere with the cultivation of the plants.

First year. After planting, the strongest cane should be pruned so it will only have three strong buds. If growth tubes are used, drive a 5 to 6 foot high stake into the soil near each vine. After emerging from the tube, the vine can be trained to the stake. To avoid girdling, tie shoots loosely or with plastic tape. Connect the stake to the top wire with a piece of twine if the lead vine grows higher than the stake during the first year. If trellises cannot be built during the first growing season, stakes should be used instead. If trellis is used instead of growth tubes, attach a piece of twine to the top wire and loosely tie it to the base of the newly planted vine. To keep the twine straight, secure the twine to the top wire with just enough force. As they develop, shoots can be attached to the twine.

Spring – second year. For the second season, your main training objectives should be to establish one or two straight trunks. If growth tubes are used, now is the time to remove them. The one or two straightest trunks should be cut back to the first live, but strong bud, at the top. Other shoots must be removed once the dormant buds have developed into 2 to 6 inch shoots. To help the plant use its food reserve for vine growth, flower clusters must be removed as they appear. Train the two shoots after they reach the top wire in opposite directions. Of the two developed trunks, choose the shorter or weaker one for removal. Train the remaining shoots in opposite directions.

Spring – third year. By this time, trunks and cordons should be established. Remove all canes that develop on the trunk and prune back the laterals on the two cordons to two bud spurs during dormant pruning. The cordons should be 4 feet long if the vines are 8 feet apart. Allow all remaining buds to produce flowers and bear fruit.

Fourth year and older. Remove as much wood as possible from vigorous and productive grape vines during pruning. Many fruit clusters with small berries will result in too little pruning. Prune too much and maturity is prevented. This will result into a weak fruiting wood for next year. A mature vine will have several hundred buds before pruning and more than half of them are capable of producing fruiting shoots. Make sure that vines are pruned and not allowed to overproduce. as this will surely reduce the following year's crops. On the other hand, if vine is over pruned, it will excessively grow vigorously and bear only a part of the crop.

Time to prune. New growth may be held back if pruning is delayed during the dormant season. They will be saved from injury from spring frost. However, pruning must start early enough so that the entire vineyard is pruned properly. Late pruning may cause the occurrence of harmless "bleeding". Grapes should not be pruned in the fall after they are dormant because grapes are susceptible to winter injury. Start pruning by February instead. The size and form of the vine are modified through pruning. This modification helps in maintaining the vine's vigor and sufficient fruiting wood. Crop production is affected by both deficiency and excess of good fruiting wood.

Balanced dormant pruning. More than 75 percent of last year's growth should be removed during pruning. Growers use the concept of balanced pruning to determine fruit capacity of a vine at pruning time. Unless there are many grapes and they cannot be all pruned before April, this must be done in February and March.

Pruning considerations. To establish the starting date of pruning, decide how much time it will take to prune the entire vineyard and count back from April 1. You should wait as long as possible before pruning the grapes, because late-pruned vines have delayed bud break. This will facilitate detection of winter injury. New shoots are able to avoid late frost because of delayed bud break.

Pruning procedure. There is a simple way to prune the vines. The first step is to size the vine and estimate the weight of one-year-old wood. Select five to seven renewal spurs to be retained and make sure that they are equally spaced on the cordon. Select fruiting canes to be retained and remove the rest. The second step is to determine how many buds to leave. To do this, weigh pruning from a vigorous vine and a weak one. If too many buds remain after weighing, then prune to the desired number of buds. Because the first (and sometimes the second) bud have unfruitful shoots, start counting the buds with the second or third bud.

WATERING AND FERTILIZING

Water Utilization. Grapes need little irrigation once they have established themselves in the vineyard. The vines should be placed where they can be watered heavily and deeply, but not frequently. Bear in mind that heavy clay soil tends to hold water around the roots, which is what happens in overwatering. Too much water can trigger chlorosis, a condition that indicates iron deficiency. It is characterized by pale, small, yellowed leaves with dark green veins. The first remedy is to reduce the frequency of watering.

Fertilizer Requirements. Once the vines have been well-established, they do not need much fertilizer. They are not heavy feeders. Application of too much fertilizer results in the stimulation of wood and leaf growth instead of fruit production. To help stimulate young plants to size up for earlier fruit production, moderate amounts of fertilizers should be used during the first and second year after planting.

Excessive fertilizing should be avoided after the first two years. Doing so would result in the production of bountiful green growth, but little fruit production. Use only nitrogen fertilizer unless soil tests indicate a need for phosphorous or potassium. Apply fertilizers only if the leaf turns yellow during the early part of the season or if poor cane growth is observed. Excessive growth will be forced, resulting in fruit spoilage if application is done during the ripening period.

WEED CONTROL

Unlike trees with deeply dug in roots, grapevines are shallow- rooted and thus are more affected by weeds. To set the vine's growth for best yields, you need to control weeds. It is the single most important practice in vineyard care, especially in the early stages. It should be your primary concern in site preparation after selecting the land for your grapes. It should also be first in your list in vine management immediately after planting. Your other practices in the culture of your vines will be for naught without weed control. Once you have eliminated perennial weed growth, it is only a matter of preventing those that develop from seeds.

- ➤ Weed control can actually influence vine growth. Too much weed and crop-cover growth can reduce water availability to the vine and restrict its growth.

- ➤ Weed control practiced with crop-cover reduction increase soil water availability and, thus, stimulates the growth of the vine.

- ➤ Clean spaces around the vine also increase temperatures on sites where frost is a problem.

There are several options for weed control around newly-planted vines.

They are:
1. Manual
2. Mechanical,
3. Chemical,

4. Mulching
5. Combinations of one or more practices.

Manual. Using hoes and hand weeding is an acceptable vineyard practice and has been known to result in good vine-size development. However, there is a tendency to underestimate the difficulty of the task. Scheduling biweekly weeding throughout the growing season can make this method successful.

Mechanical. This is practiced with several types of equipment, including hilling-up/taking-out plows, offset rotovating devices, offset cultivators, etc. While this method can efficiently control weeds between vines, they do not reach the critically important weed growth immediately around the vines. This make supplemental manual weed control essential.

Mulching. There are several materials that can be used for mulching. These include strips of black plastic mulch, straw, grass clippings, shredded bark, stones and newspapers held down with stones. The use of black plastic mulch has been shown to give results no better than that obtained with the use of herbicides. In addition, there are complications in managing vineyard row middles at the edge of the plastic mulch and, more importantly, disposing of the material at the end of 1 to 2 years.

Herbicides. Weed control using pre-emergence herbicides is not an easy task. There are a limited number of available herbicides for this purpose, and many do not control a broad variety of weed species. Moreover, equipment must be obtained and calibrated to ensure proper rate and patterns of herbicide application. An added complication is that adequate rainfall after application is required to activate the chemicals.

Pre-emergence herbicides work by interfering with seed germination. It will not control existing weeds, and that's why perennial weeds must be controlled before planting. This type of herbicide is typically water insoluble, yet they must penetrate ¼ to ½ inch of the soil to be effective. For this reason, rainfall is required after application. They should only be applied after all tasks that will disturb the soil surface have been accomplished, including hand fertilization of vines and trellis construction.

Application should not be postponed for long after planting, as germination of weeds may have already begun or a late spring drought may occur. Either of these instances may result in the failure of this method. It is, therefore, recommended that vines be planted as early in the spring as possible; and then perform hilling, fertilizing, trellis construction and weed spraying in rapid succession.

DISEASE CONTROL

Diseases limit the production of grapes. There must be effective disease management for the vineyard to survive. Besides being costly, controlling them may have a negative impact not only on the environment, but on the workers and eventual consumers of the produce. A balance must be struck between use of synthetic pesticides and the maintenance of production goals.

The most common diseases are listed here.

Black Rot. This fungus attacks the leaves, stem and tendrils in the spring. Early symptoms include small brown or black spots, but cause no serious damage. The fungus then spreads to the fruit where it will not be noticed until berries are about half grown. Diseased parts should be removed and destroyed at pruning time.

Botrytis. This fungus attacks during flowering and is only apparent later in the season. Symptoms manifested are single berries turning brown and rotting; affected areas bear gray spore masses. It will not grow at temperatures above 94 degrees F. It is best controlled by an integrated program using pruning and fungicides. To help reduce infections, an open canopy is the best option as it allows air circulation to keep the fruit dry.

Grape Anthracnose. Infections are manifested as light gray centers and reddish-brown borders on fruits. Stem lesions are similar in color, and sunken with slightly raised borders. Infected leaves curl down from the margins.

Downy Mildew. Attacks all green parts of the vine. Lesions are yellowish and oily, which later on becomes angular, yellow to reddish brown spots. All infected parts except older fruit are covered with white fungal growth during moist weather. To control use pre-bloom sprays.

Powdery Mildew. Infects all green parts of the vine. Manifestations of disease include a white powdery growth on infected parts. Infected immature berries split and either dry up or rot; can cause off flavors in wine. To control this disease, spray starting at petal fall.

Phomopsis Leaf Spot and Cane Blight. Leaves have small chlorotic, irregular to circular spots with dark centers. Spots may also occur on veins and petioles. Infected fruit become dark brown and brittle. Early sprays and use of proper pruning is essential to control this disease.

Botrytis Blight. Attacks primarily at bloom, killing the flowers. Fruit may also be infected during ripening. White berries turn brown while dark ones become reddish. To control, use bloom sprays.

DISEASE CONTROL PRACTICES

These practices are **pruning, cultivating and spraying**. You must be prepared to carry out all three of these practices. Otherwise, you will not be a successful grape grower.

Pruning: Diseases that overwinter in old canes can be controlled by pruning out and burning all excess growth. The remaining vine should only contain the permanent trunk.

Cultivating: Because the fungus which causes Black Rot can also come from old berries, cultivating the soil just before new growth begins in the spring covers old berries and reduces black rot infection.

Spraying: Timely application of fungicide is the key to using sprays to control diseases. Success as a grape grower will depend on understanding of spray equipment and the application of spray material.

PEST CONTROL STRATEGIES

In order to successfully manage pests in your vineyard you need to have:

- ✓ A basic knowledge and understanding of the grapevine itself, how it grows and how it is propagated, including their hardiness and susceptibility to various pests and pesticides.

- ✓ A working knowledge of the biology and life cycle of the flora and fauna that surround your vineyard and how these creatures flourish or perish in their environment.

- ✓ Information about the cultural, biological and chemical control strategies that can be used for grape production and how to effectively apply them.

PEST MANAGEMENT

Bird Control. Common pests of grapes include several species of birds, such as the robin, starling and blackbird. They do much damage to the fruit by plucking entire berries from the cluster or by pecking holes in the berries. These birds usually begin to feed on grapes before the fruit matures and after they have developed color. As soon as this occurs, control efforts must commence.

- ➢ Bird control methods' effectiveness and cost varies. The most effective one is to cover the vines with plastic or nylon netting. The cost for the initial outlay is quite high but with careful handling, the materials (such as the net) may be usable for three to six years.

- Yet another option is to buy a light-weight plastic net for one season.

- Another relatively inexpensive, but only moderately effective method, is the use of a visual or auditory frightening device. Propane cannons, recording of bird distress calls, high frequency sound emitters, hawk-mimicking kites and balloons, and brightly colored reflective streamers can be employed. Birds become used to them quite quickly.

- Long-term effectiveness requires changing location every few days. Combining the visual auditory devices usually has better results.

Deer. These animals can cause significant damage to the vines and foliage. The most effective method of keeping deer out is the use of fences. There are several designs available, from low-cost electric spider fences to 6 wire electric ones, or 8 foot high or higher non-electric models.

Insects. There are several insect types that can damage grape vines or fruit. However, they only cause serious injury occasionally. Frequent examination of plants for signs of pest activity is one key for controlling insect pests. Control should be applied before the plant is seriously injured.

Grape Berry Moth. This is the most important grape pest. This insect overwinters on the ground in cocoons. The adult lays eggs on the flower clusters or small fruit in late May or early June. In July, the mature larva forms a small leaf flap that it folds around its body. They either remain on the leaves or fall to the ground. Each larva feeds by tunneling through three or more berries and cause them to shrivel or fall to the ground. If larvae are found, apply approved insecticide. You can use pheromone traps to help monitor flight and egg-laying periods.

Grape Leafhopper. There are several species of this insect that damage grapevines. Adults are active, wedge-shaped insects, about 1/8 inch long. They are white to yellow with yellow or orange markings. They feed by sucking juices from leaves. Leaf injury reduces vine growth and interferes with berry ripening. To monitor infestation, examine undersides of leaves for their white cast skins. Start control measures if insect populations are large enough to discolor leaves.

Grape Phylloxera. This is a small aphid-like insect. It survives on the roots of susceptible cultivars throughout the year. Heavy infestation of this insect results in premature defoliation and reduced shoot growth. After a couple of years of heavy infestation, vine vigor and yield can be seriously reduced. Insecticides for the foliar form are only effective if used when nymphs are crawling on the outside of the leaf. The best time to spray is during the bloom-vine stage.

Cutworms. These insects cause serious damage by cutting off the developing canes, especially very early in the season. Damage occurs commonly in weedy areas. Weed control can reduce injury to plants. Approved cutworm bait is the most effective way to control this pest.

Chapter 5 – Vineyard Management

The difference between maintaining a successful vineyard and handling a failing one is seen in the quality of the grapes produced. Success is based not just on one factor, but a string of the best practices implemented by the grower and associates from day one to the harvesting of the vines. While it can be a difficult and challenging task, the rewards are more than just sweet grapes.

Knowledge and expertise requirements. Growing quality grapes require a high level of knowledge and understanding of all things related to the grapevine business. Among other things, a grower should know:

- ✓ Grapevine physiology and morphology because it helps in understanding how they grow and what factors affect their development, whether it be good or bad.

- ✓ The varieties of cultivars and how they differ from each other, and what particularly productive cultural practices are applied in their cultivation.

- ✓ The biology of diseases and pests that attacks the plant, how they multiply, survive and become injurious and destructive to the plants.

Having these in mind, the grower can plan the strategies to combat the threats besetting the vineyard. Striving to have continuing education will carry the budding grower a long way to the table of success.

MANAGING VINEYARD ROWS AND AISLES

Vineyard management has many aspects. You start by:

1. Surveying the site and taking into consideration the factors that will determine the row orientation, spacing between and within rows.

2. In laying out the rows, turning space should be provided for the tractor or any equipment used in the training, pruning and harvesting process.

3. Will you be using mechanical means for these or will it be by manual labor?

4. It is also important to look at the irrigation system to be implemented, as well as the drainage system, if required. The choice of one system or method will certainly influence your next choice of subsequent processes.

Vineyard Design and Layout. The optimal layout of a vineyard is usually in straight rows. A North-South direction is best, as this orientation intercepts the maximum amount of sunlight. In sloping land, however, this cannot always be followed as this type of land may require contour planting of straight rows across the slope. You can obtain information from the USDA Soil Conservation Service and State Extension Specialist on how to design vineyards on sloping sites.

> Soil erosion is common on such sites, so to prevent erosion, contour planting is

implemented. However, it often leads to other problems such as trellis design and construction. It might be more economical and practical to divide the vineyard into several sections to deal with differences in the topography and soil type.

➢ The training system preferred, and available equipment, defines how the rows are spaced apart. A commonly used measurement is nine to ten feet between rows, although this may be increased to 11 to 12 feet if larger equipment is used, and for sites with steep slopes or for divided canopy training systems. For most commercial operations, rows spaced less than nine feet apart are generally too narrow. Wider row spacing accommodates easier operation of equipment, harvesting and pruning. One drawback, however, is the fact that this reduces the number of plants per acre, thus affecting yield per acre.

➢ The expected vigor of a particular cultivar influences the relative spacing of vines within the row. The usual practice is to provide spacing of 8 feet for most American and French hybrid cultivars, and 6 feet for cultivars with lower vigor. Vines, once matured, should completely fill the trellis space, while at the same time; avoid competition against other plants for sunlight. The distance between vines could be reduced. This will result in the increase of buds per unit area and lead to increased yield. However, shoot crowding and shading will reduce the productiveness of the vines.

- Rows must be parallel along their entire length. You can use a tractor mounted pole twice as long as the row spacing. Begin by attaching three marking teeth to the pole, one in the center and one at each end. Drive the tractor along a well-marked base line to start. Mark additional rows by following a previously marked one during consecutive passes. Leave enough room, like 30 to 40 feet, at the end of the rows for turning equipment.

- Another way to lay out the rows is to use a 100 foot tape measure, marking flags and spray paint to mark the ground. Choose a baseline and establish the first row. Additional rows are marked off starting with this initial row. Use the right triangle rule to make sure that row ends are marked perpendicular to the first row or baseline. Take steps to ensure that a true 90 degree angle is measured. Otherwise, rows will not be spaced correctly. You can also use a transit to shoot exact angles.

- If you are planning to use mechanical methods to prune and harvest the grapes, then it becomes doubly important to have the vines in rows accurately spaced. This is to avoid damage to vines, trellises and equipment while working in the vineyard. In this light, the use of laser-powered levels and laser guided planters has become more common.

PRUNING GRAPES

The point of pruning is to have control over the vines so that they remain productive for many years. Unattended, like in the wild, grapevines tend to become unruly. They have the ability to grow and spread to cover a sizeable area. They can produce more vegetation that is needed and is right for them to develop into mature plants. Under such circumstances and without management, fruiting will be poor and grape quality inferior for the coming year.

DEFINITIONS

> *Pruning* is "the removal of plant parts to obtain horticultural objectives".

These objectives include:
1. Controlling the size and form of the grapevine.
2. Optimize the production potential of the grapevine.
3. Maintain a balance between vegetative growth and fruiting.

> *Training* is "the arrangement of plant parts spatially". This is done to develop a structure that:

1. Optimizes the utilization of sunlight and promotes productivity.
2. Adapts to the characteristics of the grape cultivar.

3. Promotes efficient and sustainable vineyard management practices.

4. Is economical to establish and maintain.

The need to prune. How you would prune your grapes is determined by the training system you have chosen at the beginning of the planting season. There are training systems that by the nature of their physical structure lend themselves to mechanical pruning; while there are others which need more skilled labor, but are not suitable for mechanical pruning.

The point to remember is that an unregulated vine produces huge crops. If you have not done any pruning the previous year, you would have left buds on the vines and this means a bumper crop of grapes for the following year. However, having been allowed to bear so much fruit, the vines can't generate enough energy to bring those fruits to the ripening stage. Fruits produced this way will have poor quality, and not worth using at all.

- Pruning actually removes as much as 95 to 98 percent of the growth from the previous season.

- This helps to keep the vine in a balanced condition by regulating crop size. It is a vital process that actually adjusts the quality of the fruit.

- Through pruning, the vine's growth is controlled so it will be easy to manage.

➢ These points have to be attended to if you are to grow quality crops.

PROPER PRUNING OF GRAPEVINES

1. For one year old canes that grow along the cordon, pruning is done so that they are reduced to either three to five node spurs as fruiting wood or one-node renewal spurs as vegetative wood.

2. The diameter of the cut end of the spur should be at least pencil size. Vegetative shoots are produced from renewal spurs and are used in the next year's fruiting wood. It takes around three years for grapevines to be considered as mature and fully productive.

3. By late February through March, dormant pruning should have been completed. For the previous summer's growth (all one-year-old wood) pruning is done so as to leave three to five nodes per spurs, which should be evenly spaced along the cordon.

4. The number of buds to retain for fruiting is dependent on how much vegetative growth there was the previous year. There are several approaches to determine the number of fruiting buds. At least 85 to 90 percent of the one-year- old wood will be removed during dormant pruning. This is done so that grapevines are able to maintain their shape, have the fruit load distributed correctly along the cordons and keep the fruit quality high.

Approximately 40 to 50 buds should be left on three-year-old, or older, vines.

Pruning tools. As with any project, appropriate tools should be used to effectively remove all undesired wood from grapevines. These tools include:

- ✓ Loppers
- ✓ Hand pruners
- ✓ Handsaws.

For heavy two-or-three-year-old wood, use a lopper or saw to cut through. They should be handled properly to do a job as cleanly as possible to avoid unnecessary injury to the vine.

CLUSTER THINNING

Flower-Cluster Thinning. To control crop load, flower cluster thinning is done. It is the manual removal of some of the flower clusters on each shoot. This should be done when the clusters first appear.

- ➢ Cluster thinning is effective in increasing the vigor of very weak vines, and in reducing excessive crops on vigorous ones.

- ➢ Timely reduction in crop load will result in larger, earlier ripening fruits that have higher sugar content than over-cropped vines. It is a common practice to leave one cluster per shoot.

Some growers use growth regulators to control fruit size. Gibberellic acid is a natural plant hormone usually produced by seeds. Most seedless grapes respond to gibberellic acid with an increase in berry size. Some cultivars, however, react negatively to the hormone. On the Canadice, for example, the increased berry size can result in excessive compactness and berry cracking. Concord seedless also have a negative reaction. Gibberellic acid is applied at mid bloom and at fruit set, usually about 7-10 days after bloom, to reduce berry number and increase berry size.

A reduction in bunch rot in seeded cultivars with very compact clusters can be achieved with gibberellic acid by reducing cluster compactness. For such types of cultivars, the acid is applied when shoots are 4 to 6 inches long. Care must be taken when applying gibberellic acid because some seeded cultivars vary in their response. Misapplication can result in increased winter damage and reduced bud fruitfulness for the following year.

Training Systems and Cluster Thinning. As mentioned above, the pruning method to apply is dependent on the training system used. Leaf removal to enhance exposure of clusters to sunlight is difficult and inefficient when the training system places clusters in a random orientation on the trellis. Only those training systems that place the grapes in a well-defined zone are compatible with the use of leaf removal. Shoot positioning is suited to those training systems that have shoots originating from a structured, predictable location on the trellis. Some training systems are in fact more effective when used with such practices. For example, shoot positioning is essential to obtain the full benefit of the Geneva Double Curtain training system.

CANOPY MANAGEMENT

The grapevine canopy consists of the shoots, leaves and fruit. It is important to create a harmonious interrelationship of these elements so that the grapevine will produce fruits with the desired properties.

In a well managed canopy,

- Shoots are of medium diameter, with moderate length internodes and few lateral roots.

- Shoots are normally spaced about 3 inches apart and have around 15 normal sized leaves and length is about 3 to 4 feet long.

With the correct training system, the canopy with the best characteristics would have most of its leaves well exposed to sunlight, with good air circulation. Such a canopy promotes abundant fruitfulness and good ripening. These characteristics provide the best defense against fungal disease development.

Vine balance. It starts with a good vineyard design, which includes:

- ✓ Correct vine and row spacing and
- ✓ Use of the appropriate training and trellis system.

Balanced pruning is practiced to maintain a good balance between vegetative growth and fruiting.

- Balance is achieved when the vine has a canopy of adequate leaf area to support the intended crop load to the desired fruit ripeness.

- A balanced vineyard is one whose vines have enough room for growth and fruit production.

- A vineyard is out of balance when it has overly vigorous, dense and shaded canopy, or excessively weak with inadequate leaf area.

Once balance is achieved, the vineyard does not require much of canopy management. You only need to maintain it by standard pruning, some shoot thinning, and shoot positioning as required by some training systems. Vines possessing low vigor should be examined. These vines could be competing for water with weeds or a cover crop. There could be inadequate irrigation or over-cropping. Diseases, insects or poor soil condition could have damaged the root system or trunk. Correction of these problems should improve the vine's vigor to a more desirable level.

Over-irrigation or too much rainfall can lead to vines with excessive vigor. Close vine spacing will also result to an overly vigorous vine that can occupy more than its allotted space on the trellis. In regions with low rainfall, improved irrigation management may improve vine balance. To regulate soil water availability, cover crops that compete with the vines can be planted in the alleys. Caution should be exercised however, to avoid excessive competition with the vines.

MANAGING VIGOR AND QUALITY

A standard practice for managing vigor and quality that depends on some training systems utilized is shoot positioning. Through positioning, shoots are arranged in a manner that displays most of the leaves to sunlight.

Shoot positioning on high trellis systems. This is usually practiced on high vigor vines using the double curtain training system. It may also be done with single curtain vines to obtain better positioned canes. Shoots are usually positioned so that they don't form a "solid mat" on top of the cordon. Canes that grow along or cross the top of the cordon are repositioned so that they flow downward. This should be done only after shoots have become strongly attached and when canes begin to change color from green to brown. It is common to start this practice in early to mid July and may be repeated after 30 days.

Shoot positioning on low cordon systems. Cultivars with an upright to semi-upright growth, adapt well to the low cordon system and vertical shoot positioning, which consist of tucking the canes between the sets of catch wires as they develop. This practice often requires several trips around the vineyard throughout the growing season.

Shoot Thinning and Suckering. Extraneous shoots should be removed early in the season. At this time they can easily be broken off. To balance the canopy and improve fruit quality, thinning of weaker primary shoots should be done. The target spacing is about 3 inches between shoots. It is important however, to avoid excessive shoot thinning particularly in high vigorous vineyards as removal of too many shoots stimulates rapid growth of the remaining shoots during the flowering period. Suckers that originate from the base of the trunk should also be removed because they will grow up into the canopy and will contribute to crowding.

Hedging. This refers to the topping or summer pruning of the grapevines applied to non-shoot positioned training systems such as the high cordon. This is done to shorten long shoots or laterals. It is also commonly practiced on vertically shoot-positioned vines when they become too long to be supported by the trellis wires. Use long knives to manually do this or use a tractor mounted machine. Consider that vines respond to hedging as it stimulates lateral shoot growth, especially for vigorous shoots, requiring repeated hedging.

Leaf Removal. To increase fruit exposure to sunlight and improve air circulation around the clusters, it is recommended to do leaf removal. This practice also facilitates good spray coverage for efficient disease control. Leaf pulling is usually done immediately after fruit set. This is important for fruit development as they need to be exposed to sunlight very early and become acclimatized to high sunlight conditions. Sun burning will happen if done very late. Do this only on the east or north side (depending on row orientation) of vines to avoid direct sunlight exposure during the warmest time of the day.

Vigor Diversion. Use of vigor diversion canes is a recommended method to reduce canopy density and shading, especially for excessively vigorous vines. In this method, one or more extra canes are retained at pruning time. This extra cane, sometimes called "kicker" canes, greatly increases the total number of buds per vine. These kicker canes are allowed to grow until about mid season and then are cut off at their base and removed from the vineyard. The difficult part of this system is to find a way to hold the kicker vines away from the fruiting canopy to avoid interference with spray penetration or shading the canopy.

Change Training System. Converting to a divided canopy training system can best solve the problem of having chronic over-vigorous vines. In the Geneva double curtain and Lyre system, for example, canopies can be divided horizontally. This type requires wide row spacing. For a vertically divided canopy system, the better choice is having narrower row spacing, as in the Scott Henry System and the Smart-Dyson Ballerina system.

Chapter 6 - The Start

THE START

Wine is the product of the fermentation of grape juice and the creativity of the winemaker. Grapes pass through a lot of steps before you can taste its sweetness (or whatever characteristic is present in it) **Winemaking** or **vinification,** as it is known, is not only a science but an art as well. It is a natural process that requires very little human intervention. Yet when humans do intervene, embellishing, improving, or even deviating from one or more parts of the process, the result is wine at its best.

Wine begins its life through the fermentation process. It commences when yeast is added to grape juice. As the yeast consumes the sugar present in the grape, it converts the sugar to alcohol and carbon dioxide.

The grapes you have produced in your vineyard will have its own identifiable characteristics, as it is with all the other grape varieties. However, the style and personality of the wines are created by you, the winemaker. You will direct the winemaking process, imparting your mark on the finished product.

There are five basic steps to winemaking, namely:

1. Harvesting,

2. Crushing and pressing

3. Fermentation,

4. Clarification,

5. Aging and bottling.

Countless variations exist within each step. This makes winemaking the more interesting. Each deviation actually makes each wine unique.

Winemaking involves the management and optimal control of the process of fermentation, as well as aging and storage. The following are the processes within the fermentation stage that the winemaker should be aware:

- ✓ Type of juice (or grapes) and yeast
- ✓ Sugar content
- ✓ Acid level
- ✓ Fermentation containers (i.e. oak barrels)
- ✓ Exposure to air
- ✓ Process for clearing wine
- ✓ Temperature / humidity
- ✓ Ageing

By optimal selection of key ingredients and processes, excellent wine can be made from juice! We shall be dealing with all these steps and processes later.

THE SPACE FOR WINEMAKING

The superior grapes you produced in your vineyard intended for winemaking will amount to nothing if you don't have the proper wine storage facilities. Correctly storing the wine in a room with stable temperature and humidity will allow it to age properly and maintain the best bouquet and flavor.

Temperature – The optimum temperature for a wine cellar is 50 to 55°F (10-12°C). However, any constant temperature within 40-65°F (5-18°C) will do. Drastic temperature fluctuations must be avoided as cool temperature retards the ageing of wine; while a warm cellar poses a higher risk of spoilage for the wine, as well as make it age faster.

- A slow change of temperature of ten or so degrees is not a problem unless it happens on a daily or weekly basis.

- Damage to your wine will be noticeable from the sticky deposit that often forms around the capsule.

- Subject to frequent and long temperature fluctuations, the wine expands and contracts and, as it does, it damages the integrity of the cork. This allows tiny amounts of wine to escape and make its way alongside the cork, allowing some oxygen to enter the bottle.

Humidity. A relative humidity range of 50-80% is acceptable, but around 70% is recommended. No harm will be done if humidity exceeds this point, but it may cause rotting in other paper products like labels and cardboard boxes stored in the room. A high-humidity room also provides moisture to the cork and helps keep it stable and elastic. Insufficient humidity on the other hand may cause the corks to dry out, lose their flexibility and allow air to get into the bottle and ruin the wine.

Darkness. Wine exposed to light will age prematurely. Clear bottles are, of course, subjected to this problem. However, even dark-colored, glass bottles can be penetrated by ultraviolet light, which may give an unpleasant aroma to the wine. Sparkling wines are more sensitive to light than other wines. Incandescent or sodium vapor lights are preferred for cellars rather than fluorescent ones.

Calm. Vibrations and excessive sounds that create vibrations from machinery or any source disturb the sediment of the wine and can, thus, be harmful. Wines should not be moved around. Once it is laid down, it should stay that way until it is ready to be opened and consumed.

Cleanliness and Ventilation. The cellar should not be subjected to foul smell and debris. Smell can enter through the cork and spoil the wine. This can be avoided with good ventilation. Debris, on the other hand, could harbor insects that might infect the corks. Fruits or other food products that are capable of fermenting should not be stored in the cellar together with the wine.

Angle of Storage. Wine bottles are stored horizontally. This allows the wine to be constantly in contact with the cork (for cork-topped wine bottles) so the cork is always kept moistened and doesn't end up being distorted as a result of drying up. This keeps the bottle air-tight, preventing oxygenation. Storing the bottles with labels up will facilitate observance of the sediment deposit that forms on the opposite side of the bottle when it is opened.

Your home's basement might be the ideal site for this. But while this setup may not be available for most home brewers, a rather more expensive option is to use an electricity powered wine refrigerator. This setup guarantees stable temperatures so you will be sure to obtain the optimum temperature for aging your wine.

TOOLS FOR WINEMAKING

For the serious beginner and home brewer, it's always best to start with a winemaking kit. Because the kit comes with everything needed, winemaking is fun and so much easier.

If you are more adventurous and like to put up things yourself, you can create your own winemaking kit (available from commercial winemaking kit stores) that contains most, if not all, of the following:

Primary Fermentation Buckets. The purpose of the primary fermentation bucket is to keep the must contained during fermentation and to keep all other foreign matter out of the wine.

- ➢ It should have a lid that is big enough to contain the volume of crushed grape you want to process.

- ➢ Some primary fermenters are available with airtight seals and rubberized o-ring holes in the top. This is where an airlock can be fitted.

> Some come with a tap at the bottom for draining off the wine after fermentation. Some winemakers avoid these types because after the primary fermentation is over, a thick layer of sediment usually forms at the bottom and this will clog the tap.

You must be sure that bucket is a food grade plastic, preferably without prior use.

Airlocks. An airlock is a device attached to a container that lets gasses come out but not in. This is important, especially during the slower, secondary fermentation, usually done in a carboy. It keeps the air out but allows the carbon dioxide to escape. There are two major types:

1. **Two-Piece Airlocks** – recommended for vigorous fermentation where the contents of the carboy or primary fermentation bucket could spew out into the airlock.

2. **"Bubbler" Airlocks** – recommended for easier-going, secondary fermentations.

Whichever type is used, they need to be checked frequently to make sure water is still present. One major cause of spoiled wine is a dry airlock. Instead of plain water, a weak solution of sodium metabisulfite could be used to keep away insects.

Secondary Fermentation Carboys. This is a big glass bottle that resembles the bottles used in bottled water machines. Usual sizes are 2.5, 3, 5 and 6 gallons. With the carboy, you will need a long handled brush that fits into its mouth and reaches the bottom.

Carboys must be sanitized before use and before storage.

> **Alternatives to Glass.** You can use plastic as a secondary fermentation vessel. However, bear in mind that some winemakers say that the plastic imparts off flavor to the wine.

CHEMISTRY TOOLS

1. **Acid test kit to measure total acidity (TA).** TA is measured by the process called "titration", which involves adding one liquid to another a bit at a time until change in color is observed. The pH meter displays a numeric value representing completion of the titration process without the need to guess when the color change has happened.

2. **A triple-scale hydrometer to measure the specific gravity of the wine.** A unit of measurement is called a "brix". The device will show measurements as specific gravity and as the percent of alcohol measurement in your wine.

3. **A pH meter to measure pH level.**

RACKING TOOLS

The process of siphoning the wine from one container to another is called racking. This leaves the sediment that has accumulated in the original container. These sediments, called "lees", are the by-products of fermentation such as dead yeast cells. The wine should not be left sitting for too long since it can pick up off flavors from them.

This is basically a plastic hose, one end of which is placed down into the wine in the original carboy and the other end into the carboy where the wine will be transferred, usually located on a lower level. You suck in slowly on the tube that's on the lower level carboy until the wine is halfway down the tube. Once wine flows freely, you must immediately get it inside the empty carboy as fast as possible. You might get a few mouthfuls on your first attempts so you might want to practice with water beforehand.

Alternatively, you can use a siphoning kit purchased from a brewer's supply store.

MEASURING TOOLS

There are times when you may need to add ingredients to adjust certain characteristics of your wine. This process is called "amelioration". It is important to accurately measure the quantity of these ingredients.

- ✓ **A Kitchen Scale**: To measure ingredients, such as sugar, by weight. It is essential that you have a scale that is accurate to the gram.

- ✓ **Measuring Spoons**: you could use either plastic or stainless steel. Included in the set should be a ¼ and 1/8 teaspoon measures.

- ✓ **Beakers and Flasks**: glass containers used to test the wine with. These are particularly useful if you are using a pen-style pH meter.

- ✓ **Pyrex Measuring Cups**: in 1-cup, 2-cup, 4-cup, and 8-cup sizes.

- ✓ **A Floating Thermometer**: this type of thermometer is weighted to stick up above the must in the primary fermentation vessel. It's used to monitor temperature of fermentations.

WINE PRESSES

A wine press is used to press the last of the wine from the grape skins after the primary fermentation and before the secondary fermentation. The cheapest type is called a basket press. It has a basket that holds the wine skins and pressure is applied by screwing a top piece down to compress them. You can also use a nylon mesh straining bag if you don't have a wine press.

BARRELS

In modern wineries, wine only spends a few months in oak barrels, the primary purpose of which is to impart the special taste of oak to the wine. For home winemakers, extra care must be taken as they risk overpowering the more subtle flavors of the wine with a heavy oak taste.

There are alternatives to barrel aging such as oak chips, oak tubes, oak staves and oak dust.

BOTTLING

This can be done with minimal equipment, such as a siphon hose (which could be the same one you used for racking). You can siphon the wine from the carboy where you have been bulk aging the wine into the bottles. You can opt to use commercial bottling equipment instead. Bottles must not be overfilled, as the cork may not want to go in. Under filling on the other hand will leave enough air in the bottle capable of spoiling the wine.

CORKERS

There was a time when winemakers used a rubber mallet to drive the cork into the bottle. Nowadays, however, you can buy a quality hand corker. These corkers squeeze the cork to make it thinner as they insert it into the neck of the bottle leaving it at just the right level. Corks can fall into the bottle if pushed to far and it can be difficult to uncork. Corks left sticking out above the bottle do not look good at all. A good corker will do it just about right.

WINE MAKING INGREDIENTS

The following ingredients play a specific and distinctly different role in the vinification process.

- **Yeast Nutrient:** Provides energy for the yeast and insures that that your yeast will ferment and make alcohol in sufficient quantities.

- **Pectic Enzyme:** Added to help break down the fruit during fermentation. It also aids in extracting more flavor and body from the grapes, as well as, ensuring that the wine will clear up successfully.

- **Acid Blend:** Used to help control the wine's sharpness. Many wines will not have enough acid on their own, making the wine taste flat or flabby.

- **Wine Tannin:** Added to increase the character of the wine and helps in its clarification after fermentation. It also aids the wine to take better advantage of aging during storage.

- **Wine Yeast:** The ingredient that actually does all the work. It turns the sugar in the juice into alcohol.

- **Campden Tablets:** Added before fermentation, and again before bottling. They insure that your wine does not spoil and remains fresh tasting up to the point of consumption.

Chapter 7 – Picking Grapes for Wine

When to Harvest. Harvesting is usually done in the fall. There are three important determining factors for the grower to make this decision:

- ✓ Sugar levels (brix)

- ✓ Tannin development (seed color and taste) and

- ✓ Acidity

Then there is also the weather to account for. It determines whether a year is going to be a "good vintage" or not. Proper timing of the harvest is essential because of its effect on grape composition. Harvesting grapes prematurely will result in thin, low-alcohol wines. If done very late, wines with high-alcohol, but low-acid content, will be produced.

How to pick grapes. There are two ways to harvest the grapes. They can be picked either by hand or by machines. Growers choose one over the other for different reasons. Machine harvesters are quicker, but have the disadvantage of indiscriminately picking up of foreign non-grape material in the product, especially leaf stems and leaves; and, also, depending on the trellis system and grapevine canopy management, moldy grapes, canes, metal debris, rocks and even small animals and bird nests. Hand picking is more time consuming and costly, but will yield a better product selection. It has the advantage of using skilled labor to not only pick the ripe clusters, but to leave behind those that are not ripe or have defects.

Machine picking. Most machines hover between the grape rows, shaking the row they are riding directly over. This action causes the grape bunches to drop over a conveyor belt that carries them through a chute to a ton crate being pulled by a tractor on a nearby row. There are large grape farms that usually own a grape picker. For a fee they will accept harvesting the grapes for smaller farmers. Instead of buying your own machinery, consider hiring someone to harvest your grapes for you, as its price may be worth it. If you are going to use a machine picker, care should be taken when making sharp turns and driving up steep inclines. If you find that a slope is too steep to drive up, stop. It's safer and better to handpick the grapes instead.

Hand picking. This method is always preferred for harvesting wine grapes. You need grape cutters or pruning shears to cut the bunch from the vine, and clean picking containers. You will also need adhesive bandages and antibiotic ointment just in case you injure yourself while doing this. Place the bunch of grapes in the picking container, like a basket or any other suitable container. Do not throw them down because you will risk breaking the skins, losing the juice and attracting insects. If you are going to stack the containers, make sure that those on top do not crush the grapes in the containers below. It is best to pick grapes in the morning and do the processing in the afternoon. Store them in a cool place as much as possible. Before processing make sure you remove the rotten fruits.

RIPENESS OF GRAPES

One determining factor for grape ripeness is color change. However, there are grapevines that do change color long before they change their flavor. As they become fully ripened, the natural bloom or whitish coating on the berries should become more noticeable. For their part, the seed's color changes from green to brown.

Another factor is the size and firmness of the berry. Most grapes should become slightly less firm to the touch when they become ready. But this varies depending on the cultivar's individual characteristics.

The most effective way to tell the ripeness of the grape is its sweetness. Tasting them directly picked from the vine is best. While other fruits continue to become sweeter even after being picked, grapes don't. After they are cut from the vine they will not ripen any further. Thus it is important to make sure grapes are in the right point of sweetness before you harvest. The right amount of light that reaches the plant's leaves determines fruit quality. This helps the fruit to ripen and develop good color, as it is in the leaves that sugars are manufactured and transferred to the fruit.

There are years when some grape growers report uneven ripening, particularly with concord grapes. This condition usually occurs in warm years. Uneven ripening means that some of the berries in the cluster are sour, hard and green while most others develop the color purple and soften during the ripening process. In some cases, the berries are full-sized but lack sweetness. There is no clear explanation for this phenomenon, but warm weather is partly to be blamed.

Harvested grapes can be stored for possibly up to eight weeks, depending on the cultivar and storage conditions. The ideal temperature is at 32 °F with 85 percent relative humidity.

SUGAR

Grapes have high sugar content, usually 20 percent when ripe. Most grapes contain about equal amounts of glucose and fructose.

Grapes develop in four distinct stages:

1. **Green stage** – at this point, the green berries grow rapidly by cell division. Little sugars develop, although acids begin to accumulate.

2. **Rest stage** – cell division is slowed down considerably, as well as the growth rate.

3. **Veraison stage** – here the berries change color and soften. There is an increase in berry size by expanding cell volumes. The acid levels decreases; but water, sugars, aromas and flavors increase.

4. **Dehydration stage** – at this stage, the berries soften and some may have slightly wrinkled skins. Sugar production is halted, but brix may continue to increase slowly as the berries lose water. For most winemakers, it is better to pick white grapes late in the veraison stage (20-23.5 brix), but will choose to pick red grapes early in the dehydration stage (23.5 – 25 brix).

ACIDITY

One of the major components of wine that affects balance is acidity. Enologists divide acidity of wine into three categories:

1. **total acidity** – takes into account all of the acids in wine.

2. **pH** – a quantitative assessment of fixed acidity, which is measured as total acidity minus volatile acidity.

3. **volatile acidity** – its amount is small compared to total acidity; it is closely associated with quality; its measurement indicates spoilage.

A perfect balance of these three components will result in the best wines.

ACID/pH ADJUSTMENTS

It could happen that grapes will have less than ideal pH and acid balances. In this case, there is a need to adjust the acid and pH levels.

Reasons for adjusting the grape acid level:

- ➢ The pH is too high and the acid too low;

- ➢ The pH is too low and the acid is too high;

- ➢ Both the pH and the acid is too high, usually the result of excessive amounts of malic acid and potassium.

The second and third are common in grapes growing in cool climates; although the third could also occur in warm climate grapes.

A maximum of pH 3.3 is the ideal level for all white and rosé while reds should have a maximum of pH 3.4 for these wines to achieve optimum flavor extraction and to minimize bacterial infection. These adjustments must be made with tartaric acid. The normal measurement for tartaric acid addition is 1 g/l to reduce pH by 0.1. Bear in mind the following:

1. Not all grapes have the same buffering capacities;

2. High pH drops, from 3.6 to 3.3, for example, may require about 4 g/l of tartaric acid instead of the usual 3 g/l.

3. Some precipitation of potassium hydrogen tartrate may result when acid is added. Lab tests should be performed to determine if this is happening.

All the acids - tartaric, malic and citric - will affect the TA values differently, thus affecting the flavor differently, too.

There may be some instances when acid reduction prior to fermentation is required, particularly if the season has been unfavorable. This can be done as follows:

Water addition. The addition of ten to fifteen percent water will give the desired TA without making significant changes in pH. Sugar will have to be added, however, because of dilution.

Cold stabilization. This is done usually after fermentation when the temperature is slightly below freezing. The wine can also be placed in the refrigerator as an alternative. This helps to "seed" the wine with cream of tartar crystals. This process will not work if the pH is too low, (less than 3.2) because the malic acid content will be higher that the tartaric acid content. Cold stabilization also reduces the probability of tartrate precipitation.

Calcium Carbonate (CaCO3) or Chalk. Seeding with cream of tartar crystals and chilling hastens the process. This will not work, however, if the pH is too low. It should be done well before bottling, at least three months prior, or a chalk haze or crystalline deposit could occur in the bottle. Because this process takes a long time most wineries do not prefer this method.

Potassium Carbonate (KCO3). The wine should be chilled, although it will work at cellar temperature. Potassium carbonate reacts immediately and does not leave a deposit.

Malolactic Fermentation (MLF). Malolactic fermentation removes malic acid. It converts malic acid into **lactic** acid. One gram of malic acid is converted into 0.67 grams of lactic acid and the rest is given off as **carbon dioxide**. There are two reasons why it is employed: 1) It is a natural means of reducing acidity; 2) As a stylistic tool, it changes the character of the wine by making it softer and slightly buttery.

Blending. Many winemakers prefer blending high acid wines with low acid wines to balance acid. Because it doesn't use any chemicals, it is considered to be safe and yields immediate results. The process involves doing an MLF on a portion of the wine and blending it with the non-MLF portion. This is to balance the softer lactic characteristics with the more aromatic and fruitier characteristics of the grape, which in turn, results in a more complex wine.

Index of Acidity (IA) or Acid Taste Index

Acid balance is a matter of taste. There is no set rule that determines the correct acid balance. Research has been done, however, that gives some general guidelines to determine if acid balance is within the desired range for the type and style of wine. The formula is to simply subtract the pH from the TA. For example, dry red wines should have an IA range of about 2 to 3, dry white wines should have about 2.7 to 3.7 an off-dry white wines about 3.8 to 4.8. IA's below these levels will result into flabby or soapy tasting wines, while those far above them will have wines that are sharp and acidic.

These numbers are general guidelines and may be useful as tools to help achieve good pH/acid balance. However, the final arbiter of proper balance is the taste buds.

Chapter 8 – Basics of Wine Making

BASICS OF WINEMAKING

The art of winemaking has centuries of history behind it. It has evolved from simple homebrews from grapes harvested from backyard vineyards of old, to big modern wineries producing thousands of bottles each year. Barefoot grape stompers have faded away and were replaced by machines that efficiently extract the juices from the grapes.

Fermentation used to be left to Mother Nature to finish the entire process of converting the must to the best wine. Now, it can be controlled and enhanced, allowing it to mature until it possesses the desired qualities. From harvesting to bottling, the wine has to undergo a process not dissimilar to diamonds in order to come out with the best aroma and flavor to delight wine drinkers.

ASSESSING OF MUST

Must means "young wine" in Latin. It is freshly pressed grape juice that contains the skins, seeds and stems of the grape. The solid portions of the must is called pomace which usually makes up 7% to 23% of the must total weight.

Straining the must. One way to ensure success of winemaking is to carefully strain the liquid from the fruit pulp. The goal here is to allow as little solid matter as possible into the vessel for the anaerobic fermentation. You should avoid squeezing the pulp through a straining mesh or bag. Doing this will convert the flesh of the fruit into puree and will pass through the wine. Always try to apply gentle pressure on the flesh. You can use coarse, medium and fine nylon mesh sheets ideal for straining solids from liquids.

> Straining and filtering are different from each other.

> Straining is removing the coarser particles of solid matter from the juice.

> Filtering wine is to pass it through a very fine sieve with microscopic perforations in order to remove all suspended matters and leave a clear liquid.

Must weight. It is a measure of the sugar content in unfermented grape must, indicating the amount alcohol that could be produced once it has undergone the process of fermentation. It is a tool to help winemakers predict the finished wine's potential alcohol content

> Must weight is usually measured by using a refractometer or a hydrometer.

> To quantify must weight, three scales are used: baumé, brix and oechsle.

Must weights are usually measured in the vineyard. They provide the state of ripeness of the grapes, which is a big help when selecting the time of harvest.

ALCOHOLIC FERMENTATION

In winemaking, alcoholic fermentation, also known as primary fermentation, refers to the conversion of sugar into carbon dioxide gas and ethyl alcohol. It reveals the hidden quality of the grape – especially the aroma. It starts as soon as the sugary grape juice is exposed to the yeast. Fermentation will continue until all the sugar has been consumed and converted to alcohol or the alcohol level in the juice has reached around fifteen percent, whichever occurs sooner. The yeast will die naturally and any leftover sugars will remain in the wine until the alcohol level reaches around fifteen percent.

Fermentation requires two things: **sugars and yeasts**.

1. **Sugar.** The level of sugar in the grapes from which the wine is made determines the level of alcohol in the finished wine. The presence of more sugar means more for the yeast to work on and convert it to alcohol.

    a. A technique called chaptalization is done to boost the level of alcohol in the wine by adding sugar to the juice at the time of fermentation.

    b. Some wine recipes recommend adding sugar in portions throughout the fermentation process rather than mixing it all in the beginning. This is quite true if the intended product will contain a high level of alcohol.

2. **Yeast.** There are many varieties of yeast strains coming from different places. The type of yeast used contributes significantly to the aroma of the finished wine.

a. The most common type used is *Saccharomyces Cerevisiae*. This type is also used for beer fermentation and for bread leavening.

b. In the initial stages of fermentation, yeasts do an aerobic respiration, meaning they use the oxygen present in the must, transforming the sugar into water and carbon dioxide. After all the oxygen has been consumed, the real fermentation stage begins. The yeast at this point does the process under anaerobic conditions, which is without oxygen. They produce energy by oxidation of sugar and transform it to ethyl alcohol, carbon dioxide and other secondary product.

MALOLACTIC FERMENTATION

Also known as MLF, malolactic fermentation is a very natural process. It is done by certain types of bacteria capable of metabolizing malic acid leading to the production of lactic acid and carbon dioxide. It lasts usually from a couple of weeks to three or four months under certain conditions such as:

➢ The amount of malic acid present in the wine

➢ The strength of the culture

> The conditions under which the fermentation is allowed to occur

EFFECTS OF MALOLACTIC FERMENTATION IN WINE

Thousands of malolactic bacteria exist, some of them having better effects on wine than others. While some wineries will choose to use one strain over the other, the desired result for all types is a wine that is softer in taste and has greater complexity. Red wines usually undergo this process, while it is discretionary for white wines.

Winemakers will usually elect to have this process applied to a particular wine for the following reasons:

> **To add stability to a wine:** Bottled wines can go through uncontrolled MLF and can become cloudy with sedimentation and slight carbonation. This risk can be eliminated by putting the wine through MLF with the appropriate strain of malolactic culture.

> **To lower the acidity of a wine:** Grape juice may have a high acid content due to several conditions such as climate, time of harvest, etc. Letting the wine undergo malolactic fermentation can effectively reduce the overall wine acidity.

> **To alter the character and flavor of a wine:** After going through the process of MLF, wines tend to be less fruity in flavor and aroma. This, however, is replaced with a

deeper, richer and more complex character. A creamy texture with slight hint of buttery to vanilla flavor can be noticed.

Malolactic fermentation is usually applied to the big, heavy red wines such as Pinot Noir, Merlot and Cabernet. White wines, on the other hand, are considered to be inappropriate for an MLF.

RACKING

Racking simply refers to the process of siphoning the wine must from one container to another clean secondary container (usually a carboy). Doing so leaves all the sediments, also called lees, behind in the original container. This is the sole purpose of racking, although it also helps clarify the wine and enhance flavor. It is an important step because as the wine sits and finishes its secondary fermentation, the dead yeast and lees fall to the bottom. This sediment imparts a bad taste to the wine so it is wise to remove it. However, it is okay to leave the wine with the lees for three months, as long as the lees are stirred every week or so. This way no off flavors, off odors or hydrogen-sulfide gas can form. Wine is actually improved.

> Racking is done when necessary. As long as there are fresh deposits on the bottom after a regular interval of 30 to 60 days, but not less than three weeks, the wine should be racked. The wine can be ready for bottling only after this interval has passed and there are no fresh lees, and the specific gravity is 1.000 or lower.

The wine's exposure to oxygen-laden air must be minimized. One way to ensure this is to sparge (sprinkle) the carboy with carbon dioxide or argon gas before racking the wine into it.

> Attaching a racking wand to the racking hose can facilitate the job. It is an L-shaped plastic tube that allows better control where the bottom of the take-up is located. The take-up end is fitted with a protective cover that helps prevent the hose from sucking the lees below into the receiving secondary container.

> You can also attach a racking clip to the mouth of the carboy to hold the take-up end of the wand at a predetermined height or depth.

ROLE OF OXYGEN IN WINE MAKING

Exposing the wine to oxygen will cause oxidation. Oxidation affects both the color and the taste of the wine. One common example of this process is its effect on an apple core exposed to air for a couple of hours. The apple core turns brown and the taste is not really good.

How Does Oxidation Affect Wine? Wine exposed to oxygen will turn brown, the same way that the apple did. White wines will exhibit an amber tint and red ones will manifest a brown edge. In extreme cases, the wine can develop a nutty to caramel aroma and may also develop slight off-flavors that taste like raisins or worse, cough syrup.

> Oxidation affects white wines more easily than red wines. The main reason is because reds have more color pigmentation than whites. This acts as an anti-oxidant that

preserves the wine's color and flavor. Another reason is that it is easier to observe discoloration in a white wine than in a red.

- Oxidation must be avoided in all phases of wine production. One such phase is when wine is exposed to air during racking. Wine is splashed during siphoning, and this actually is inviting air to get into contact with the wine. To prevent this from happening, make sure you fill the container being siphoned into from the bottom up, which is putting the siphon hose in the very bottom of the container to be filled. This way, only the first bit of wine coming out of the hose will touch air.

- Another source of oxygen exposure comes from improper long-term storage of wine. This type of oxidation is slow and affects the wine's character irrevocably. This usually happens during long time bulk aging of the wine after completion of the fermentation process. Air contact should be kept to a minimum. Thus, head spaces in containers need to be reduced. This can be done by moving the wine to a more appropriately sized container or topping the wine up with water or another finished wine of similar style.

- It should be noted that both light and heat will speed up the effects of oxidation. As recommended in a section above, wines should be stored in a cool, dark area.

Another way to reduce oxidation is to add a dose of sodium bisulfite or campden tablets right before aging or bottling.

Doing so will release sulfur into the wine and drive out most of the oxygen present. It also fills any small head space in the container with sulfur gases and reduces air exposure. Adding ascorbic acid, an anti-oxidant, will also help reduce the effects of oxidation.

ROLE OF SULFUR DIOXIDE IN WINE MAKING

While still on the vine, grapes are covered with yeast, mold and bacteria. Yeast turns sugar in the juice into alcohol and carbon dioxide in the fermentation process. Yeast also gives the wine a distinct flavor.

However, the yeast present on the grape skin before being harvested may not have the desired flavor, and the other things present are not good for the wine. Those unwanted elements can be eliminated using the most common and "universal disinfectant" called sulfur dioxide.

All wines contain sulphur dioxide in different forms. They are collectively known as sulphites. But the sulfites which remain in the wine may cause a lot of discomfort to some of those who drink the wine. Therefore, some winemakers prefer not to do this and let the wines be subjected to the whims of nature and develop different flavors, depending on the yeast that has been in the grapes. But even in totally unsulphured wine, traces of it are present at concentrations of up to 10 milligrams per liter.

Three reasons you might want to avoid adding sulphur dioxide to your wine.

1. **Taste**. SO2 has an unpleasant taste and smell.

2. **Health**. It can cause potentially fatal allergic reactions and has been linked with other health problems.

3. **Principle**. Adding SO2 does away with the naturalness of the wine.

USES OF SO2 IN WINEMAKING

- For must of white wine: to avoid activation of alcoholic fermentation and to allow decanting of the solid parts.

- Before beginning alcoholic fermentation so you can select the yeasts you prefer; and in the case of red wines, to allow a better extraction of color and tannins from the skins.

- To avoid oxidation and development of unwanted bacteria or yeast when the wine comes into contact with air.

Effects of Sulfur Dioxide. These can be classified into four categories:

1. **Antioxidant** – prevents oxidation of coloring substances, tannins, aromas alcohol and iron. There is a high risk of oxidation every time wine is exposed to air, which is practically any phase of production. It is even higher when the must or wine is rich in enzymes or molds. Use of SO2 can limit the effects of oxidation and ensure higher quality and keeping of wine.

2. **Stabilizer** – SO2 retards the development of bacteria responsible for malolactic fermentation. In must obtained from white grapes, it delays the start of fermentation which allows the decanting of solid parts and lets the must to become limpid.

3. **Solvent** - It favors the extraction of some substances existing on grape skins. In red grapes, SO2 allows the extraction of coloring substances and tannins during the maceration of skins in the must.

4. **Effects on taste and aroma** - Sulfur dioxide prevents the oxidation of fruit aromas in young wines. It attenuates the tastes of rot and mold. To obtain these positive effects, SO2 is added when the alcoholic fermentation is completed. Adding it too early can result in the development of unpleasant tastes and aromas.

Adding sulphur dioxide in the winemaking process is indispensible and essential. However, its use should be limited and in the least possible quantity. Its judicious use can result into the making of the best wines.

Chapter 9 – Making White Wines

MAKING WHITE WINES

White wine, although universally recognized as such, is in fact more yellow than white. The process to produce white wine is more delicate than that of red wine.

There are two methods for producing whites:

1. Using white grapes. The resulting white wine is from the fermentation of the must from white grapes only.

2. Using red-grape variety. This is more complex and seldom done. The must obtained from red grapes is cleared of skin, stems and seeds, which must absolutely have no contact with it because they contain the coloring substances.

HARVESTING THE GRAPES

The time to pick the grapes for white wine production depends on the variety that was planted and the desired style of the finished wine. Timing is important as they need to be picked at the right time of the day to ensure the right balance between acids and sugars. To prevent bruising, the grapes are picked carefully. They are first placed in a cleaner that removes foreign non-grape matter.

Some types of grapes are more acidic than others and need more time on the vine to produce more sugar. Other varieties that are destined to be produced with lower alcohol content do not need the same amount of sugar during fermentation. White grapes tolerate cool climates better than reds.

However, during harvest time, they can easily suffer from too much acid.

On the other hand, many warm-climate Chardonnays have too much sugar, and, therefore, potentially more alcohol when ripe. Picking them when they still have low sugar content would result in inadequate flavor.

As they approach ripeness, some grape varieties have their acids drop drastically. Due to this, some winemakers decide to pick the grapes while acid levels are still reasonable, even though flavors are still undeveloped. They simply add acids, often at the crusher, so they may have more flavor.

As far as diseases are concerned, white grapes have a higher tolerance against infection without compromising quality. An infection of "dry" botrytis can, in fact, improve wine with many varieties.

They need to be picked not only at the proper time in their life cycle, but also at the right time of day to ensure the acids and sugars are all at the right balance for the wine. The grapes are picked carefully, to prevent bruising, and often first put into a cleaner that removes spiders and leaves (and, one winemaker told us, occasionally mice!).

SORTING

Grapes are harvested as whole clusters in the vineyard. Because of this, many other non-desirable and foreign matters are also picked up. When the grapes arrive at the winery, they are sorted for quality. Grapes destined to be made into white wine skip the destemming process. Whole cluster pressing of white varietals accentuate a more delicate flavor, fruitiness and aroma. However, destemming white grapes can add greater tannin extraction and more body.

JUICING

Immediately after their arrival in the cellar, the grapes are crushed. At this point, all skins and stems are removed. The resulting juice (free run must) is sent to settle in containers. The rest of the grapes are pressed as quickly as possible. As air is the enemy of white wine, contact with it must be minimized because during oxidation, the wine becomes colored. The must from pressing is added to the free run must.

TREATMENT OF JUICE

The particles and impurity of the grapes separate from the must after 6 to 12 hours. These are removed through racking of the must. It is then made ready to be clarified, after which the clarified juice is poured into a tank, ready to start fermentation.

Juice Clarification. Prior to fermentation, the usual way to remove bits of solid matter from white grape juice is by settling. Twenty four hours is the standard period of time to sufficiently clarify the juice. Normally this is done at cold temperatures, although, this means a slower process. In large wineries, a centrifuge is used to do the job.

RACKING AND BENTONITE FINING

Racking. White wines are usually racked shortly after the completion of alcoholic fermentation. It is repeated after the wine has been hot and cold stabilized.

Bentonite. Bentonite is usually added to white wines for clarification fining and to remove excess proteins. All wines contain proteins of different types, but in wines with little tannin, some of these proteins coagulate and form a granular precipitate when warmed. This makes the wine hazy. No damage is done to the wine and the sediment formed is odorless, but a hazy wine is not good to look at and may offend consumers.

One to two grams of dry bentonite per gallon of wine is the normal dose. Excessive amounts can strip desirable aromas from the wine, so it is important to do bench testing. Bentonite must be diluted with water and allowed to stand for at least 24 hours. It should be added to the wine slowly and must be stirred continuously. It has a major disadvantage though: it produces large quantities of lees, which are light and fluffy, making it difficult to rack. The point to consider is: if the wine is cloudy or too tannic, then fining has to be done.

FERMENTATION

After extraction of the juice, the liquid is held in a stainless steel vat. Here, the yeasts turn sugar into alcohol. Winemakers have a choice whether to use the naturally occurring yeast that are found in the grapes or use cultured yeast. The fermentation process generally takes from 3 to 4 weeks.

The ultimate goal of fermentation is to keep finesse and the quality of aroma. This can only be achieved with a thorough control of the temperature range during the process, usually between 60 degrees F to 68 degrees F. This range will allow the optimal aroma development, including the slow transformation of sugar and an excellent production of alcohol. The fermentation process can stop and is made difficult if lower temperatures are allowed to persist. On the other hand, higher temperature will make fermentation overactive, resulting in the loss of refined aromas and you will get a coarse and ordinary wine.

Since fermentation produces heat, temperatures easily rise above 68 degrees F, especially during mild seasons. The best way to cool the fermentation tank down is to run cold water along the sides of the tank. To counteract cold temperatures, lukewarm water may be used instead.

POST FERMENTATION

Cold stabilization. After the completion of fermentation, the wine now goes through the process of cold stabilization. Here the wine temperature is dropped to almost freezing to precipitate out the tartaric crystals, also called "wine diamonds" that can form. The purpose of cold stabilization is to remove all these crystals. The crystals are natural products of the wine and quite harmless, and the process itself can hurt wine flavor, but it is done so consumers will not panic when they see crystals in their wine bottles.

How is it done? Tartaric acid and potassium occurs naturally in grapes so they cannot really be removed. The problem is that these form crystals in the wine bottles, and if this happens while the bottle is already in the consumer's home, everything is lost. So to avoid this, winemakers forces all crystals to form right there at the winery.

The main stainless steel fermentation vat usually has a cooling system worked into it. After fermentation, that vessel is allowed to almost freeze for 3 to 4 days allowing the crystals to form. These crystals cling to the sides of the vessel and remain behind when the wine is removed.

SWEET WINE

Sweet wine is produced by grapes having more sugar than the yeast can actually convert to alcohol. In the normal vinification process for white wine, a dry base wine is produced, which in cooler countries, is perceived as tart and acidic. The white wine produced this way was sweetened by adding some unfermented grape sugar, known as "sussreserve" or "sweet reserve". The product is a light refreshing wine.

The most notable sweet wines are those made from concentrating the sugar in the grapes that gives a natural and luscious sweetness with just the right acid balance. An infection of the fungus "botrytis" or "noble rot" actually enhances this process as the fungus shrivels the grapes and consequently concentrates the sugar.

Making sweet wines. Sugar added at the start of the fermentation process has nothing to do with how sweet the wine will eventually turn out, as this sugar will only be turned into alcohol.

If the fermentation went as usual, the end product will be dry, i.e. without sugar or close to dry as the process is completed. Sweetening can then be done, according to your taste. To prevent any re-fermentation, potassium sorbate, a stabilizer should be added. By adding your beginning sugar in this way and then sweetening later on, you have complete control over the sweetness and final alcohol level of the wine.

Sweeteners. One important thing to remember is that after adding sugar to wine to sweeten it and the fermentation has been completed, it is important to add wine stabilizer at the same time. Not doing so may make the wine restart the fermentation process all over again, causing it to become dry.

It is quite okay to use regular, store-bought, refined, cane sugar; but there are other sweeteners that can be used as well.

Corn Sugar may not be as sweet, but it seems to impart a crisper and cleaner flavor to the wine, making it lighter and more delicate.

Rice Syrup gives a character that can best be described as minty.

Honey is also a good choice.

Wine Conditioner is heavy syrup with stabilizer already mixed in. It makes sweetening the wine a simple procedure.

Juice concentrates is another appropriate choice and one that enhances the wine's flavor

Fresh fruit juices can be used in the same way as concentrate.

Artificial sweeteners should be used with caution, as some do not bond well on their own with liquids. Soft drink makers use binders to keep these artificial sweeteners suspended. Wine sweetened this way that has been stored will need to be stirred up off the bottom before serving.

Chapter 10 – Making Red Wines

MAKING RED WINE

Red wine gets its color from the skins of the grapes. They are fermented in contact with solid materials from the grape, like the skin, seeds and pulp, in order to extract the compounds that give the wine its color, body, and depth of flavor and aroma. For sure, among the many types of wines, red wine is among the best.

PICKING THE GRAPES

The making of a good red wine starts by having the grapes perfectly ready for picking. They must only be harvested at the proper time of their life cycle to ensure that acid and sugar levels are at the right balance. The condition of the berries when they were harvested is quite crucial to obtaining the best quality wines. This potential can be undermined by picking at the wrong time. The optimal ripeness of the grapes is very important.

- Under-ripe red grapes will have low sugar content, thus possessing low flavor and low color and will be inappropriately high in acid. Wines made from these grapes are substandard and can be overly tart because of the high amount of acid. It can be removed either biologically or chemically, but any acid adjustments should be made before the start of fermentation.

- Red grapes can only be considered ripe if they have the correct amount of sugar, acid, color and good varietal character and flavor intensity. Overly ripe ones have high sugar content, low acid, high color and excessive "red fruit" flavor. Wines made from these grapes are high in alcohol and may taste flat or bland because of acid deficiency. This condition can be corrected by the addition of tartaric acid to the must prior to fermentation

SORTING, DE-STEMMING AND CRUSHING

De-stemming refers to the removal of the stems from the grape bunches (at least 90%). Crushing of the grapes refers to the process that exposes the juices to the yeast for fermenting. They don't need to be mashed, just sufficiently split to allow the yeast in to do their work. It also exposes the skins so that they can give color to the wine during the primary fermentation.

This particular step in red wine making can be accomplished manually by squeezing the grape bunches over a grate with holes. The juice goes through, while the stems are left behind.

> ➤ The old fashion way of doing this is to "stomp" with your feet on the grapes and remove the stems later. This is the stage where you can adjust the acidity of the wine.

If you have a lot of grapes to crush, it might be good idea to use a crusher/de-stemmer instead. Do not confuse this with a wine press. Its primary purpose is to just crush the grapes so that the juice comes out. This is a device where unwashed grapes are directly added to the top hopper on the machine. The rollers crush the grapes and let them fall through the grate below, down into the fermenting container. The "destemming bar" ejects the separated stems out of the unit. The juice, skins, seeds and pulp that go into the fermenting container is called "must". Adding yeast to this will start the fermentation process.

FERMENTATION

Although fermentation is a natural process, it will not be successful if any native wild yeast and bacteria on the grapes are not removed prior to the addition of your special winemaking yeast. These unwanted elements can start the fermentation alright; but, in the end, they generally produce some terrible off flavors and aroma in the wine. Additionally, some of these wild yeasts are intolerant to high alcohol levels and may stop fermenting before all sugars have been converted into alcohol, thus creating a "stuck" fermentation, compromising the whole batch of wine.

- ➢ To avoid this potential ruin, sulfite is added immediately after crushing to eliminate those errant yeasts and bacteria. The amount applied is just enough to kill (or at least inhibit) spoilage organisms.

- ➢ If the grapes you have are in good condition, use 50 ppm of SO_2 based on the total volume of the must.

- ➢ If they are not, add more sulfite to combat the presence of mold and bacteria, up to 100 ppm.

Bear in mind though that SO2 levels above 50 ppm inhibits Malolactic Fermentation. The 50 ppm dosage at the right moment in crushing is generally okay.

To assist the action of the yeast, you must maintain the temperature around 25 degrees C to 30 degrees C, and ventilate the must regularly. If the wine's temperature falls under 25 degrees C, it will not have enough body; if it rises above 30 degrees C, the wine will be too tannic.

This stage goes on for 4 to 10 days until the maceration process followed by the malolactic fermentation.

MACERATION

This is the stage where the tannic elements and the color of the skin disperse in the fermented juice, giving the wine its body and color. For new wines, the maceration process is very short. They are supple and contain little tannin. Those that are destined to be kept long need a lot of tannin, so they undergo a long period of maceration, perhaps several days or even several weeks.

PRESSING

During fermentation, the wine extracts everything it needs from the seeds and skins. After its completion, it is time to press. This should be done in a timely way because a continued and prolonged contact with solid contents might cause undesirable off-flavors and thus, ruin the wine.
Pressing includes straining the liquid off then squeezing the remaining skins and seeds to get the wine out. A nylon mesh bag or a food grade bucket can be used, as well as a

real wine press that you could purchase or just rent for the day.

There are two design types of presses:

1. Traditional ratcheting basket presses – they work by pressing the pomace (the solid parts, such as seeds and skins) from the top of the holding basket down by using a heavy, cast iron, ratcheting mechanism. One drawback in its use is that it is very easy to get harsh and aggressive characteristics from over-pressing.

2. Bladder presses. They work by expanding a bladder using a garden hose's water pressure. The bladder is located at the center of the press and squeezes the grapes from the inside out in an even fashion. They are really gentle on the must and produce wines with higher quality. They may be more efficient to use, but are usually more expensive than the traditional basket press.

To get the fermented grapes into the press, you can scoop them out of the fermentation vessel using a small bucket and pour them into the press. Do this for small volumes. For larger volumes you can use a must pump. It is a large diameter pump with a rubber impeller to pump the must into the press. You can also employ a suction tube to remove the liquid wine from the fermentation container. Afterwards you can then shovel the skins into the press.
FREE-RUN AND PRESS-RUN:

As the must is transferred to the press, some portion of the liquid will run through the press even before you apply any pressure to the pomace. This is called **free-run.** This often produces a better wine.

The portion that is actually squeezed out of the skins is called **press-run.** This is not as good as the free-run, because the squeezing action itself extracts some of the harsher tannins from the seeds and skins.

It is, therefore, a good idea to press lightly and taste the run-off frequently so you can monitor the end point for each press. It will be different for each batch of must. The most common sign that you have reached the end point is wine with thin taste and astringent quality.

TRANSFERRING PRESSED WINE TO A STORAGE VESSEL

The pressed wine is then transferred to a temporary storage container. You can simply pour the wine using a food grade bucket with a handle or a pump, usually, into a carboy. The carboy must be filled almost to the top, as this will minimize the surface area that is exposed to any oxygen in the headspace. As the wine may expand due to temperature changes, you have to leave a space 1 – 1.5 inches below the stopper. If you are using tanks instead, and it is impossible to fill to the top, make sure that you flush the headspace with inert gas to protect the wine from oxidation.

SETTLING

After crushing and the primary fermentation, wine needs to be stored, filtered and aged. For some types, wines will also be blended with other alcohol. Depending on the winemaker, wine is stored in cellars or above ground in stainless steel temperature controlled tanks. Other similar tanks may be used where wine is stored during the settling process.

When primary fermentation is completed, the wine will be crushed again and racked into another container for the malolactic fermentation stage (discussed later). The wine is then transferred to other settling (or racking) tanks, where it will remain for one to two months. During settling the weighty unwanted debris settle to the bottom of the tank and are usually removed when the wine is transferred to another container. The settling process produces smoother wine. Some wine types may require further settling.

After the settling process, the wine is made to pass through several filters or centrifuges, where it is stored at low temperatures or where clarifying substances trickle through the wine. It is then aged in stainless steel tanks or wooden vats.

MALOLACTIC FERMENTATION

After the primary fermentation is completed, the wine must undergo another type of fermentation. This time, the harsh and tart malic acid present in the wine is converted to softer-tasting lactic acid and carbonic gas. This process is called malolactic fermentation, shortened to MLF.

The bacteria responsible for this are the lactic acid bacteria, which consume malic acid to produce energy. It is initiated by an inoculation of desirable bacteria, such as Leuconostoc, and Pediococcus bacteria cultures, to prevent other bacterial strains from imparting off flavors into the wine. This fermentation is obtained in a tank for a few weeks at a temperature between 18° and 20°C. Wine that is going through this process is cloudy due to the production of diacetyl, a substance which lends a buttery flavor to it.

Wines that go through this process tend to have a rounder, fuller mouth feel as it loses its harsh and acidic edge. Its color loses some of its vividness; and its aroma is, richer and more vinous, mellow and full-bodied.

Due to microbial instability, malolactic fermentation can occur unintentionally even after the wine is bottled, especially if it is unfiltered. Strains of bacteria convert the wine's residual sugars into lactic acid, acetic acid and other unwanted byproducts. The result is a turbid, slightly-carbonated wine that has a bad flavor. This is completely different from what is known as spritz. It is for this reason that MLF should be conducted. MLF ensures microbial stability.

CONDITIONS CONDUCIVE TO MLF

- ➤ The single most important factor is the pH level. The ideal level for red wine for developing a starter is above 3.3 up to 4.0. Some lactic acid bacteria will work well below this pH.

- ➤ Temperatures above 20 – 30 degrees C are best. The optimal time to inoculate the must is when the wine is about 1/3 through yeast fermentation, as this process generally maintains that range of temperatures.

- ➤ Low alcohol level is preferred, which is also within the above-mentioned time of inoculation.

> Unclarified wine is also preferred because it contains nutrients.

> Low SO2 levels, usually between 10 and 20 ppm are also necessary. This is also the amount added during crushing or settling.

IMPORTANCE OF USING MALOLACTIC CULTURE

As malolactic fermentation can occur naturally under uncontrolled conditions, it is better to induce it using a culture. Wild malolactic bacteria can ruin an otherwise perfectly fermenting wine.

When to initiate MLF. The rule of thumb is at the end of primary fermentation. This is important because if malolactic bacteria ferment in the presence of sugar and most of the nutrients have been used up by the yeast, the bacteria could degrade the sugar and volatile acidity may ensue. MLF can be monitored using paper chromatography. It tracks the appearance of lactic acid and the disappearance of malic acid. The presence of tiny carbon dioxide bubbles indicates ongoing malolactic activity. MLF is complete once the bubbles cease. This should last from one to three months.

Malolactic bacteria causes a pH shift. Before MLF, a pH tester will reveal a number of around 3.1 to 3.4. At its completion, you will discover that the pH has increased, indicating that the wine has become less acidic. A pH of 3.6 is the upper limit.

It is important too to check and make sure that all the malic acid has been converted. A simple test using a kit will help you do this. Once confirmed that conversion is complete, it's time to rack the wine and add some sulfite. It can now be allowed to age.

Chapter 11 – Elevage

ELEVAGE

Élevage is a French term that literally means "raising. In winemaking parlance, it refers to a set of wine farm operations that aims to improve wine taste by clarification, incidental oxygenation, and changing the wine chemistry. Generally, it denotes all of the procedures after the primary alcoholic fermentation stage up to the time of bottling. It also commonly refers to the time the wine spends in the barrel.

AGEING PROCESS

This term is reserved to be used in describing changes in wine composition after bottling. It refers to a set of reactions that improve the taste and flavor of a wine over a period of time. The final bottle bouquet is the result of many reactions during this phase.

The term wine "maturation" refers to changes in wine after fermentation and before bottling.

Wine is aged according to a plan followed by a winery and is determined by its desired style. There are wines that don't require a long period to develop and have no need for extended maturation and ageing time. Those wines are produced for early consumption, with their quality peaking in a relatively short period. They are commonly out for consumption within a year. There is no benefit in ageing them longer.

Premium expensive wines, on the other hand, acquire a complex flavor profile during maturation and develop a pleasant bottle bouquet. These wines mature best in oak barrels. Oak seems to complement the varietal aromas. The wines they produce are rich, full bodied and complex.

The following factors allow wine to age:

- ✓ **A fairly high level of tannin.** The tannins either come from the grapes themselves or from being aged in wood, usually oak. Grape tannins are more subtle, but may be as strong and rarely astringent as oak tannins. They are also better than oak when it comes to ageing. Grapes with thicker skin tend to have better ageing potential.

- ✓ **Acidity to keep it fresh tasting.** The acidity primarily comes from the grape itself, although it can be added. It can be balanced in the process but the best wines have a perfect balance of tannin, fruit and acidity in the grape itself.

- ✓ Acidity and tannin may both be present, but it is the grape that makes wine taste good, and if there is not enough of it in the wine, then it will taste like nothing when it ages.

CHANGES IN WINE DUE TO MATURATION AND AGEING

Many significant, but subtle, changes occur in the wine during the maturation and ageing period. In some cases, they are so small that they are barely noticeable, while others are quite magnificent. The most obvious change is in the color of wine. In white wine, it becomes golden then turns to brown if wine is aged too long. In red wine, purple and violet colors are replaced by orange and brick red.

Aromas change from a grape-derived odor to a more complex and pleasing one. Astringent and harsh tasting becomes smoother and rounder. The intermingling of taste and aroma yields complex, rich and delicious wines.

COLOR

The most visual and appealing properties of wine is its color. While denominated as white wine, its color is actually light yellow. At the maturation stage, when the wine is exposed to air, this color becomes darker and may even turn brown. These oxidative reactions involve several phenolic compounds. To minimize these effects, white wines are usually subjected to minimum oxygen exposure. Other reactions such as the Millard reaction and sugar caramelization also contribute to color change in white wine.

The bright red color in young red wine is due to monomeric anthocyan pigments. They are extracted from the skin during fermentation. During maturation, however, these pigments are slowly replaced by the polymeric form, a combination of anthoycyanin pigments and tannin.

TASTE AND MOUTH FEEL

The correct maturation and ageing process will help the wine become mellower and smoother, and acquire a richer mouth feel. It will also be less astringent and softer, improving the wine's sensory appeal. One more factor that contributes to improve taste is the loss of acidity due to acid precipitation and ester formation.

AROMA

Changes in aroma include the loss of certain grape or yeasty aroma, retention of the varietal aroma, and acquisition of new aromas and most significantly, all flavors, are integrated and produce a harmonious and pleasant fragrance.

TEMPERATURE

Temperature plays an essential role in wine maturation. Elevated temperatures accelerate the ageing process, but this results in significant loss of quality and complexity. In order to age the wine slowly and perfectly, a temperature of 55 degrees F must be kept. Higher temperatures can dry out the corks and make them move up the neck of the bottle. This leaves an additional headspace and thus, there is more air contact area with the wine that accelerates the oxidation process. Dried out corks can also cause leaks that further aggravate the oxidation problem. The chemical reaction rate taking place in the wine is doubled for every 10 degrees Celsius of variation. It is not good to have the wine's temperature fluctuate up and down with changes in daytime and nighttime temperatures.
Higher temperature may be useful for certain wines, but its wide scale application seems doubtful.

BARREL AGEING

There are three factors that determine the use of barrels in winemaking.

1. Wine type and style
2. Economic
3. Aesthetic

Wines that are destined for early release and are meant to be consumed young; oak barrel ageing is seldom recommended. It may not even be necessary for some styles. Light and fruity whites, aromatic whites, picnic style roses and blush, red nouveaus and some inexpensive fruity red are examples of these wines. For premium red wines with good body, complex flavor, supple texture and long finish, ageing in oak barrels is highly recommended.

Oak barrel ageing greatly contributes to the wine's richness and flavor complexity. The aromatic compounds found in oak integrate well with the wine's intrinsic aromatic fineness and sufficient complex structure. Ordinary wines cannot be turned into quality wines by oak ageing.

The use of oak barrels certainly adds to the cost of wine production. Included in cost computation are other factors such as barrel storage, maintenance, barrel exhaustion and loss of wine due to evaporation, leakage, and occasional spoilage. If your winery can make a profit with higher production cost, then it makes economic sense to use barrels for ageing red wines.

Oak barrels neatly stacked add to the aesthetic appeal of the cellar where the wine is displayed and sold. This experience can lead to wine sales and so can justify having barrels even if it is only for display purposes.

TOPPING UP AND RACKING

Every time wine is subjected to racking, a small volume of liquid is left in the original container. Thus, an air space is created in the lower container which needs to be topped up with water or wine with similar strength and flavor. Doing this avoids oxidation of the wine.

It may seem that topping up with water will dilute the strength of the wine. But this is not the case. If the pulp was strained off correctly during the first racking, loss of wine should be so small that topping up has an insignificant effect on the overall strength of the wine. If it occurs that a very thick sediment forms during fermentation, the wine may be topped up after racking with a similar type of wine. You can create a "neutral" wine from grape concentrate that can serve the purpose of topping up your wine.

Subsequent racking should result in a very little loss of wine, and topping up with water has an insignificant effect on the strength of the wine.

BLENDING AND FINING

The primary function of blending is to help in the consistency of wine from bottle to bottle. Blending cancels out any variation created from year to year from a number of sources, such as

- Differences that exist from more than one vineyard;
- Differences that develop from one fermentation vessel to another;
- Different tannin levels between barrels.

Another reason is to keep the non-varietals consistent from one year to the next. This requires more ability for the winemaker, as it involves deciding on taste and blending their way to creating the wine that matches what was produced previously.

To achieve the desired taste, different batches of wine can be mixed before bottling. If you think that there are inadequacies in a certain batches of wine, you can correct it by mixing wines from different grapes and batches, even if they were produced under different conditions. Adjustments such as adding acid or tannins, blending different varieties or vintages to achieve a consistent taste are practices that you can do.

Fining agents are used to:

> - Remove tannins
>
> - Reduce astringency
>
> - Remove microscopic particles that cloud the wines.

Fining agents work more effectively in clearing wine when a sediment base exists. It is essential to properly prepare the fining agent and to mix it thoroughly with the wine. If the fining agents fail to find enough particles to join together into larger particles, then the clarification process stalls; and if this happens, filtering is recommended instead.

The following are fining agents you can use:
Bentonite is a negatively-charged agent that attracts and brings together particles that have a positive charge. This process lets the molecular weight structures of the particles to enlarge. Larger and heavier particles fall to the bottom of the vessel when their size becomes large enough.

Egg whites are used only on red wines. You can use 1 egg per 5 gallons. You need to separate and discard the yolk, add a pinch of salt and mix it with 100 ml of water. Add this mixture to the wine while stirring it. To avoid off flavor problems, rack the wine within two weeks.

Gelatin is positively charged and precipitates with negatively charged tannin. It is a common, excellent substance to reduce tannin. You need to sprinkle 2 grams or approximately 1 teaspoon of gelatin per 5 gallons onto a small amount of cold wine or water. Soak it for 5 minutes, warm until dissolved. Add this to the wine and allow 2 – 3 weeks to settle. There may be a slight loss of color. This is not for white wines because it needs tannin to be effective, and most whites are low in tannin

Isinglass has a positive charge. It is used at the rate of 15 to 40 milligrams per liter in white wine. You need to dissolve it in ½ pint of water and shake it vigorously for a few minutes. Set it aside and after one hour, add another ½ pint of water. Shake it again and refrigerate, allowing it to set for a day or two before adding to the wine.

Sparkolloid is also a positively-charged agent. It does not strip color. If the sparkolloid is a hot mix, you need to dissolve 2.3 grams of it in ½ cup of boiling water. Simmer it for about 15 to 30 minutes until mixture is smooth and creamy. If necessary, replenish with water. Add some wine to thin and add to the wine while still hot. Mix them thoroughly and wait 1 – 2 weeks for settling. This is also available as a cold mix.

Peptic enzyme helps release the juice from the pulp when added at crushing. This increases juice yields and improves the rates of settling, clarification, fining and filtration.

Chapter 12 – Bottling

BOTTLING

Wines come to our table, bottled and labeled, all in a nice and neat little package, and ready to be served. A bottled wine's history is reflected on that bottle, impressing the wine drinker even before its flavor and aroma have started to weave their magic. Yet even then, the bottling process is still a winemaker's showcase of talent. The final stage of winemaking involves both ageing and bottling of the wine. The winemaker has the choice of either putting the wine into a bottle immediately after clarification, or have the wine undergo additional ageing. Further ageing can actually be done in bottles, stainless steel or ceramic tanks, or other suitable containers. There are a lot of options and techniques that the winemaker can choose from to employ in this final stage but in the end, it is always a matter delivering the wine with the best quality.

SO2 LEVELS AT BOTTLING

The primary reason for wine spoilage is inadequate SO_2 levels. Only the correct amount of SO_2 in wine can stop the deterioration of wine quality due to undesired yeast and bacterial activities. It also helps in the protection of wine against oxidation.

By the time your wine is ready for bottling, your main concern is to make sure that the SO_2 is at the appropriate level and that you have taken steps to prevent exposing the wine to air as much as possible during the bottling process.

Calculating the SO2 Addition. The purpose of SO_2 addition is to find out the least amount needed in order to obtain a beneficial saturation level, and at the same time avoid adding too much which will make the wine have off-flavors and foul aroma. The ideal amount is roughly 0.5 ppm molecular SO2 for reds, and 0.8 ppm molecular SO2 for whites.

> ➤ The point to remember is that the higher the pH, the more SO2 will be needed, and the lower the pH, the less SO2 will be needed to achieve the ideal level. The total amount of SO2 in a finished, bottled wine should be the least amount required but always seek to have less than 100 ppm total in the finished, bottled wine

> ➤ A sensitive palate can detect SO2 amounts over 50 ppm and too much can destroy the bouquet of a wine, eliminate delicate flavors and add a chemical taste as well.

If you don't have a pH meter, you can use ¼ teaspoon per 5 gallons for the generic level. You may actually need to use a little more or less, but this amount will have you covered.
.

Sulphur levels in different types of wine

> ➤ **Red wines** naturally contain anti-oxidants acquired from their skins and stems during fermentation, so they don't need any added Sulphur dioxide. Some conventional winemakers do add some in spite of this.

> ➤ **White wines and rosés** have no natural anti-oxidants since they were not allowed to be in contact with their skins after crushing. They are, therefore, more likely to get oxidized and

for this reason, they tend to receive larger doses of SO2.

- **Sweet wines** receive the largest doses of SO2 because sugar combines with and binds a high proportion of Sulphur dioxide added to them. To obtain the same level of free sulphur dioxide, the total concentration has to be higher than for dry wines.

BOTTLING PROCESS

Taking up the bottling process after the addition of the appropriate amount of SO2, you now have to transfer the wine into another container that will hold the wine until it is time to actually bottle it. The bottles should be rinsed, cleaned and if needed, sanitized as well. You also need to have the corks at hand and the corker ready to do its job.

Once the bottles and other tools are ready, you can start filling and corking the bottles. For filling the bottles, you can use the same racking set up that you used before, only this time, you need to attach a bottle filler to the end of the transfer tube. Fill the bottles in such a way that you leave a ½ inch of airspace between the cork bottom and the wine. This is important because leaving more airspace means having more air that could possible ruin the wine.

There are some options that you can choose from when it comes to bottling your wines. You can select the bottle's color, the type of corker to use, or even the style of the cork itself. There's also an assortment of decorative neck seals and bottle labeling to make it more exciting for you and add a professional touch to your product.

Color of the Bottle. One question to ask is whether color actually matters when choosing the bottles for your wine. There is a limited choice of color available in the market. Commercially available wine bottles come in blue, clear, smoke and amber, and several shades of green. The reason for such limitation is because wine should actually be stored in places where it is dark or there is minimum exposure to light. In this case the color shouldn't matter. But most people store their wine in the kitchen, where there is plenty of light. Light in combination with oxygen will cause the wine to lose its flavor; so if you are one of them, the best bet for you is the color green. Other than this consideration, you are free to select the color that suits your preference.

Type Of Cork: Wood or plastic? The classic wine cork comes from the bark of cork-oak trees. The bark is harvested once every several years and allowed to grow the bark back. The corks are bored out of the bark. Artificial or plastic corks are now being used more commonly than before. This is because of the stubborn problem of cork taint in natural bark corks. This is a condition that can spoil the wine by infecting it with a musty odor and stripping the wine some of its flavor. Affected wines are called corky or corked.

You can choose from any commercial wine supplies store the type of cork you want. Some of them offer different corks that suit the type of wine you have, and how long you are going to store them.

It is best to store your wine bottles on their sides if you are planning to keep them longer than a couple of months. This way, the corks remain wet, and after absorbing a small amount of wine it becomes a bit swollen and, thus, forms a tighter seal against the glass than if it were dry. It keeps air from going into the bottle and so prevents oxidation.

CAPSULES AND LABELS

A capsule or foil is the protective sleeve covering the top of the bottle. It used to be made of lead. It protected the cork from being gnawed away by rodents or infested with cork weevil. Lead capsules were phased out when research showed that toxic amount of lead remain on the lip of the bottle and get mixed with poured wine. By the 1990's aluminum has been adopted as the successor to lead as the main material for wine bottle capsules. Neck foils are usually embossed which makes the labels easy to handle. Other materials such as plastic, tin or paper are also used.

For home brewers and winemakers, wine labels bring a professional look to your own wine. Two things to consider when deciding which label to use are:

1. The color of the neck capsule on the bottle should be on the label also.

2. The color of the wine bottle itself. A green one will be more appropriate for certain labels than a blue bottle.

Information on the label. The following can be found on the label of a wine produced in the U.S.:

1. **Geographical origin:** country or state, vineyard or viticultural area

2. **Bottle size/volume:** a regular bottle of wine is 750 ml

3. **Alcoholic strength by volume**: ranges from about 8.5% to 15%

4. **Type of wine:** such as table wine or dessert wine

5. **Vintage year**: year the grapes used to make the wine were harvested

6. **Name and address of the wine producer**

7. **Specific bottling information**: where the wine was bottled; for example, estate bottled (made from grapes grown in vineyards owned by the winery)

8. **The name of the wine**: may be named after the variety of grape it was made from such as Chardonnay or Cabernet Sauvignon; or for the region where it was made; or it can be given a name created by the producer

9. **Government warning**: pertaining to pregnant women, ability to drive, and general health

10. **"Contains Sulfites":** a warning to those who may be allergic

Names of different wine bottle sizes. A standard sized bottle of wine holds 750 ml of wine. A smaller bottle, called a half bottle, is 375 ml. Bottles bigger than a standard sized bottle include:

- Magnum (= 2 standard bottles)

Page
130

- Double Magnum (Bordeaux)/Jeroboam (Champagne/Burgundy) (= 4 standard bottles)
- Jeroboam (Bordeaux)/Rehoboam (Champagne/Burgundy) (= 6 standard bottles)
- Imperiale (Bordeaux)//Methuselah (Champagne/Burgundy) (= 8 standard bottles)
- Salmanazar (Champagne/Burgundy) (= 12 standard bottles)
- Balthazar (Champagne/Burgundy) (= 16 standard bottles)
- Nebuchadnezzar (Champagne/Burgundy) (= 20 standard bottles)

Punt. Found on the bottom of Champagne/sparkling wine bottles and some still wine bottles, is a dent called a punt. Its main purpose is to strengthen the bottle, especially for sparkling wines. It is also useful for collecting sediment and for pouring wine, as it provides a place where you can put your thumb.

After you finally have a drink of your wine, you know that it is only going to get better as it ages. There are wines that need more years to achieve their potentials, while others you can be drink now and enjoy their flavor and aroma. Still, it is only with ageing that they can acquire all those extra flavors, roundness and complexity.

Chapter 13 – Types of Wines

Wine production has become a global industry comprising of many types and styles. Name brands are determined by the type of grape and where they were cultivated geographically, and the year they were produced. Needless to say, different types of grapes produce different tasting wines.

Color is generally determined by the length of time the grape skins were left in the grape juice after crushing. Red wine is produced when skins were left for a long time. White wine is produced if skins were left on for a short period. By moderating between the two, rose/blush wines are produced.

The **taste of wine** is dependent on the type of grapes from which it was made. Nevertheless, there are other factors that affect the final flavors of the wine, such as soil, exposure to sunlight and climate, not only during the entire growing season, but at the time when the grapes were actually harvested. Other factors include fermentation, types of yeast used, where the wine was aged.

In countries where winemaking is seriously monitored, the amount of a particular grape that make up a particular wine is regulated. In some US states, any wine referred to by the name of the grape (Chardonnay, for example) must be at least 75% of that grape.

Wines are not simply reds or whites. Indeed, red wines and white wines have their differences, but it is the variety of wine within each group that reveals the details about their taste. Sub-categories exist.

White wines generally go well with seafood, chicken, turkey, Chinese food and sometimes pork. Red wines, on the other hand, go well with red meats such as beef, roasts and filets, lamb, duck, veal, pastas and sausages. This rule however, is not absolute.

There are types of white wines that also go well with red meat, as there are also types of red wines that could be perfect for seafood. These generalizations are quick guidelines only developed by professionals within the wine community. You can experiment with different types of wines and food combinations.

Table Wine or Still Wine
Under US labeling law, table wine is any still, non-sparkling wine with an alcohol content of up to 14%. A wine whose alcohol level is above 14% but below 24% must be classified either as a dessert wine or as a naturally occurring high-alcohol wine. A fortified wine with a similar alcohol level may be classified as a still wine.

Fortified Wines
These are wines which have been blended with a neutral grape brandy or alcohol. The brandy may be added to either stop the fermentation process to make it sweet and retain more residual sugar (Port, for example), or after fermentation to increase the wine's alcohol level (Spanish Sherry, is one example).

Aromatized Wines
These are flavored wines which are fortified as well. Winemakers use extracts of different herbs and spices as flavoring agents. These include chamomile, orange peel,

coriander and hyssop. The ingredients are normally blended and added to a neutral base wine. The wine is then filtered after it has settled and integrated with the flavorings. These types of wines are best served chilled or muddled. The best example is Vermouth.

Sparkling wines
These are wines that contain bubbles of carbon dioxide, bottled under pressure. The carbon dioxide many result from natural fermentation, either in the bottle itself or in a large tank designed for such purpose. It can also be produced by injecting carbon dioxide in the wine.

It would be a time consuming task if we are going to list all the various types of wines made and imported from all around the globe. It will be more helpful if we take a look at a smaller sample coming from within the United States.

Wine/Grape Types	Wine Characteristics
Cabernet Sauvignon (Ka-ber-nay soh-vin-yoh)	Best known as the "King of Red Wine" it has a *deep red* color, with richness of taste and flavor. Serves well with hearty foods.
Chardonnay (Shar-doe-nay)	Known as the "King of White Wine", its color is pale to *straw yellow* producing an elegant white wine. Taste can vary from semi sweet to sour, heady or light. Goes best with poultry, seafood, red meat and cheeses.
Chenin Blanc (Shen-nan-blahnk)	Used as a blending grape for sparkling, dry and sweet wines, its color is usually *pale to medium yellow* with taste of either dry,

	semi-sweet with acidity, and goes well with chicken, seafood and fish.
Gewürztraminer (ga-VERTZ-trah-MEE-ner)	Know as the spice grape, it is a sweet *white* wine with full, fruity spicy flavors ideal with Asian foods, ham, pork and grilled sausages.
Merlot (Mer-loh)	Often used as a blending grape with the Cabernet Sauvignon grape, it has developed into a delicious wine in its own right. Its color is medium to *dark ruby*, with a plummy fruit flavor. It is a good match with beef, chicken and pasta dishes. Also an excellent compliment to chocolate.
Petit Sirah (Puh-Teet-Ser-AH)	Original produced to blend with others wines, it came it to it's own in the 1970's due to it's *red wine color* and full tannic taste. The wine goes well with beef, lamb and spicy sauces.
Pinot Noir (Pea-no-NWAHR)	Burgundy wines are most often made from the grape. Color is light to *medium red*, and darkens as the wine ages. Dishes of pasta with red sauce, light beef and fowl would do well with this wine.
Riesling (Reez-ling)	Also known as Rhine or Johannisberg Riesling, it is *pale straw* to *white* in color with a taste

	of dry tartness. It is best served with seafood and most oriental dishes.
Sauvignon Blanc (Saw-Vee-nyon-blahnk)	Another popular blending grape, its color is light to *medium yellow* with a tinge of green. Typically very light with a sweet to dry taste, it is a very popular picnic wine and ideal with fish, shellfish, and chicken and pasta dishes. In the U.S. it is also known as "Fume Blanc".
Syrah (Sir-ah) or **Shiraz** (Sear-az)	Known either as Syrah or Shiraz, the grape creates a light, medium to heavy *red color*, with taste varying from peppery to fruity flavor. Hearty foods such as beef as well as spicy Indian or Mexican foods serve well with this wine.
Viognier (V-own-yay)	A recent addition to California vineyards, it is a very difficult grape to grow and therefore grown in only a few vineyards. The grape yields a medium bodied *white* wine, noted for its spice, floral and citrus flavors.
Zinfandel, Red (Zin-fun-dell)	A very popular wine in the U.S., style can vary from light to full bodied, and color from *deep red* to *dark purple*. It has a spicy peppery flavor. Serves well with "American" foods such as burgers, pizza and red sauce dishes.

Zinfandel, White (Zin-fun-dell)	A newcomer to the wine industry, it is very popular with new wine drinkers because of its sweetness and ease of taste. Although labeled as a *white* wine, color is pale-rose and tends to have citrus and lights flavors. The wine is delicious with light sauces and pasta, fish, pork and other light meals.

Printed in Great Britain
by Amazon